Free to Believe

(Or Not)

Joy Hakim

Stories for Thinkers

Stories for Thinkers
5610 Wisconsin Ave. #505
Chevy Chase, MD 20815

Printed in the United States of America

First Printing, 2016

ISBN 978-0-9962722-9-2

Second Edition

www.joyhakim.com

Of course this book is for my five grandchildren (who I hope will read it). And for Sam, who has been unfailingly supportive and caring.

It is also for some educator friends who understand the essence of spirituality: they include Barbara Dorff, Edwin Taylor, and Juliana Texley.

And it is for Susan Neff and Heng Chao Gu, who did most of the hard work of putting this book together.

Table of Contents

Introduction

Just What is Religion?

Since this is a book about religious liberty, we need to start with a definition of religion. Just what is religion?

Is it the church you go to, or the synagogue, or the mosque, or the Friends (Quaker) meeting?

Yes, it is all those. But that is only part of it.

Religion is your basic belief system: it's how you think the world came about. And whether you think it has a purpose or not. And why you are here. And if you believe you are going somewhere from here. Most religions consider these questions. Religions also include rules of behavior and worship. Some people think religions help you answer really big questions about the universe (although some people don't agree about that).

How did the world begin? Scientists will tell you of the Big Bang theory. But what got the bang to bang?

Is there a God? Or did our world just happen? Have there been spiritual leaders—like Moses, Jesus, Mohammed, and Buddha—with special insights? Were they divine? You'll find that people disagree about that. In a nation that supports religious freedom we can discuss that issue without killing each other.

A 19th century American philosopher, WIlliam James, thought

that religion was a belief in an "unseen order" in the universe. In other words, according to James the universe is more than a meaningless collection of forces and stuff. James believed that good comes out of living in accordance with that order. Given James's definition, today's environmentalists can be labeled as religious.

In some countries citizens are not free to decide how important religion is in their lives. We have that freedom. You can make religion central to your life, or you can hardly consider it. That is a decision our religious freedom allows.

Most religions focus on the meaning of life. Is there more? Yes. Religion also has to do with the way we behave. Right behavior is called "morals" or "ethics." But who decides what is right? How do you treat other people? Do religions guide us on that? Your answers to these questions help form your belief system. And that is religion too.

Okay, religion has to do with the meaning of life and how we treat other people. Is that all? No it isn't. **Religion also has to do with the wisdom of the ages.**

Which means, just as you learn from your parents and teachers, they learned from their parents and teachers. Ideas and traditions are passed from generation to generation. Some of those ideas are in great religious books, like the Bible, or the Qur'an. Some traditions have to do with the way religious holidays are celebrated. Most religions are based on faith: religious people often believe in things that may be scientifically unprovable, like the actuality of God.

Now you may be squirming in your seat—you may be feeling uncomfortable—because you are thinking, "I

don't have a religion."

What you mean is that you don't go to a church, or synagogue, or mosque. That means you don't have a formal religion. But as long as you are a thinking person you're not left out of this discussion. Some people are secularists. They don't belong to any church group but they think and care deeply about the meaning of life and about how to behave. They have beliefs.

Atheists (AY-thee-ists) don't believe there is a God. Agnostics aren't sure about it. But being an atheist or an agnostic doesn't mean you can't concern yourself with religious issues, like right behavior. Everyone usually thinks that his or her religion, or belief, is sensible and good. Most people think theirs is the best of all. If they didn't, they'd change their beliefs.

Sometimes people from one religion try and convince other people to believe as they do. Often, throughout history, they have tried to do that convincing with swords and guns.

Religious wars have often been the most terrible wars of all. In recent years, people have died in wars of religion in Ireland and Syria and Bosnia and other places around the globe. But in this country we've avoided religious wars. How have we managed?

People here, like people everywhere, have deep differences. We don't all agree about religion. But we've found a way to live with our differences.

The men who founded this nation came up with a very good idea—a simple idea—but no nation before had ever put it into a government document. It is called **separation of church and state**. What it means is that we keep government and religion apart. We made that idea part of our Constitution in its First

Amendment (the first ten Amendments to the Constitution are called the Bill of Rights).

Before we came up with that idea of separating church and state, countries were expected to have official or state-sponsored religions and practices. Many countries still do. Sometimes people are forced to be part of that religion. We don't do that. Roger Williams, who lived in 17th century New England, said, "forced worship stinks in God's nostrils."

The First Amendment to our Constitution says, "Congress shall make no law respecting an establishment of religion." Which means the government can't establish, or favor, any religion. It also means that government money—taxes—can't be used for religion or religious teaching.

The Constitution also says that Congress shall make no law "prohibiting the free exercise" of religion. Now that is a strange way to put it.

Religion exercising? That just means that **in the United States you can exercise your mind with any beliefs that make sense to you and no one can prohibit or prevent it.** So if you want to believe, as the Norse did, in gods named Thor and Odin and Loki, no one in the United States has a right to stop you. If you want to believe, as the Romans once did, in the gods Mercury and Jupiter, go ahead. You may be a bit out of date, but that is your business, not anyone else's. In the United States you are free to believe anything you want—even bizarre things—as long as you don't hurt anyone else. President Thomas Jefferson wrote that you can believe in one God or twenty gods; it wouldn't bother him because "it neither picks my pocket nor breaks my leg."

All the great religions preach brotherhood, love, and peace, so it seems unreligious to go to war in the name of God. But it has happened over and over again. The United States has never been involved in a religious war. Many scholars believe that is because our nation does not favor any one religion; instead we celebrate religious freedom.

In the United States we don't always agree with each other. Sometimes we think other people's ideas are silly, or awful, or even dumb. It doesn't matter: we respect their right to have their own ideas. We have learned that is the best way to live with our differences. We are free to believe or not believe as we wish. And the amazing thing about this: it has helped make us a religious people. But how we express our spirituality is changing. Most Americans no longer go to church every Sunday as they once did. Most do identify with a specific religion. Worldwide, religions are in transition. The challenges of an open-information-rich world will be among the factors determining their future.

But this is not a book about religion. It is a book about how we became the first nation to legally give its citizens the right to choose any religion, or none. Before we added a First Amendment to our Constitution, nations were expected to have an "established" church supported by taxes and government leaders. We established religious freedom when we established these United States. When our states ratified the Constitution they gave up the idea of a state-supported national church. Our leaders thought that would keep our religious institutions free of the corruption that traditionally has come with state power.

James Madison was clear: "Religion and government will both exist in greater purity, the less they are mixed together."

John Adams spoke it bluntly: "Congress shall never meddle with religion other than to say their own prayers and to give thanks once a year."

Thomas Jefferson said it with eloquence: **"Truth is great and will prevail if left to herself."**

And the First Amendment made it the law of the land:

CONGRESS SHALL MAKE NO LAW RESPECTING AN ESTABLISHMENT OF RELIGION, OR PROHIBITING THE FREE EXERCISE THEREOF.

Part I

Religious Liberty

A Beginning of Sorts

The story of religious liberty in the United States began with a few small groups of people who were searching for a place to live where they could practice their religion as they wished.

Among them were Pilgrims, Puritans, and Quakers, all devout people, who were willing to leave behind everything they loved and come to a wilderness because they wanted to build a God-inspired community.

Does that mean they came to this country to find religious freedom? **Well, yes and no. None understood the kind of religious freedom we now cherish.** No country offered that. They would have been horrified at the idea of a community where there was no one religion that everyone was expected to follow. They were each convinced there was only one path to God and that they were on that path. They wanted the freedom to walk that path with as dedicated a focus as possible.

Today we think of freedom in terms of individual rights. In the United States you, as an individual, have the right to believe or not believe as you wish. The Puritans and the religious separatists would have had a hard time understanding that idea.

To the medieval mind it was the rights of God and the community that were important. Dissenting individuals, those who didn't go along with dominant beliefs, were called heretics, and heretics were not to be tolerated. Heretical ideas were thought of as dangerous. If an individual was allowed to believe an idea that was not church approved, he or she might convince others to believe that idea. And that might cause change, which could threaten the whole society. But, yes, most of these brave voyagers did come here for religious freedom. It was religious freedom as they defined it. That meant freedom to build what they saw as a community inspired by God and the Bible.

In England the Puritans were having problems with the Anglican Church, which was the king's church. They thought some Anglican leaders had political power in mind, not affairs of the heart and soul. They wanted to cleanse that church. They wanted to lead as pure a Christian life as possible. When they didn't get their way in England, some Puritans decided to build a godly community in America.

Other British dissenters didn't want to follow the Anglican way, even if it got purified. Some thought it too close to Catholic worship. Pilgrims and Quakers and Baptists had ideas on worship that were very different from the Anglicans or the Puritans. They were Separatists, with a capital "S." They wanted to separate themselves from the Anglican Church.

Most British citizens accepted the king's transition from the Roman Catholic Church to the Church of England or Anglican Church, except in Ireland, where most remained Roman Catholic. In Scotland there was a mix: some went with the Presbyterian Church (founded by John Knox), a lot of people stayed Catholic, some were supporters of the king's church (sometimes called Episcopalian), and more. This got complicated and sometimes nasty. On the European continent it got horribly nasty with Protestants killing Catholics and vice versa.

Later, America's leaders seeing all this would say: "Let's just let everyone believe as he or she wishes." How that then became law and what happened next surprised everyone.

1 Who are We? How Can We be so Different and the Same Too?

Religious Freedom in America

Khan is so tiny she must stand on a stool to see over the lectern. She is three years older than most of her classmates, but her size and her delicate features make her look much younger. Khan has worked hard to be able to stand where she is now, in front of the whole school, speaking as president of her class. Her parents are not in the audience.

It has been almost four years since the night they woke her and wept and hugged and wept and hugged again before watching as she walked off into the darkness with two men they hoped they could trust. Then they prayed that their daughter, the pride of the family, would reach the land of freedom where all were said to be equal.

The men put Khan into a small wooden boat. There she sat, scared and silent, squeezed knee-to-knee with forty others. They were lucky; they would spend only two days at sea. Pirates would take Khan's only possession of value—a gold ring, her mother's parting gift. In a camp in Indonesia, she would begin to study English.

All this happened not long after the end of America's war with Vietnam. From Indonesia Khan would fly to the United States determined to be and do all that her parents wished for her.

Standing on the podium in front of her classmates she is

already on her way to becoming an American citizen.

John, who will follow her on that podium and also give a speech, has Irish ancestors who came to America so many generations ago the family has lost count. But they, too, left weeping parents who knew they might not see their children again. Like Khan, the immigrants from whom John is descended were young when they climbed onto overcrowded wooden boats and braved the ocean's currents and the thievery of pirates.

Alex's forebears, who were on the ocean even before John's, came in chains. Captured in Africa, they were thrown, sardine-style, into a ship's hold worse than any nightmare of Hades. That they lived and grew strong and produced a class leader is a tribute to their intelligence and fortitude.

Josh, the school newspaper's editor, is a third generation American. His grandparents fled for their lives when Russian Cossacks looted and burned their village. It was because their Jewish religion was different from that of the Czar.

Juanita, a gifted artist, is the daughter of Nicaraguans who came to America so their children might find opportunity.

Fatima's father is a doctor, from India. She is a dancer: elegant and talented.

Larry, a skilled storyteller, has begun to write a novel. It is about his ancestors—people of the pueblos.

Is this mélange of young people an exaggeration? Not at all. This is an urban American school and between them, these boys and girls and their classmates are Protestant, Catholic, Jewish, Muslim, Buddhist and more. Some of them follow no formal faith.

They, or their ancestors, come from across the globe.

How did WE THE PEOPLE get this way? Read some old history books and we all seemed to be—once upon a time—white, male, English and Protestant.

Well, it was never quite so. Even at that first "English" settlement at Jamestown there were Poles, Italians, Africans—and women. The Native Americans who surrounded the colony were more influential than history has usually acknowledged.

Still, in 1787, when those words "We the People" were first written with a quill pen, the predominant power structure in the East Coast colonies was male, English and Protestant. Yet the Founding Fathers, the white men who wrote those words, saw their nation as staggeringly pluralistic. And it was. For there were Congregationalists, Presbyterians, Moravians, Huguenots,

Anglicans, Lutherans, Anabaptists, Methodists, Dutch Reformed, German Reformed, Scotch Reformed, Dunkards and Quakers, to name only some of the Protestants. Besides, there were Catholics and Jews. In Europe all those people were killing each other because of their different beliefs, and had been doing so for centuries. People being people, they could have brought their religious wars to America. They didn't. Why not?

That's what this book is all about. Something special happened here, something unique in world history. A great idea was developed and put into our founding documents. Like all great ideas it is a simple one. Here it is: government has no business meddling with people's beliefs. Here it is again: church and state should be separate. Here in the words of James Madison: "The religion... of every man must be left to the conviction and conscience of every man."

2 Why Here?

Now you may be asking yourself, why did Khan, Alex, John, Juanita and so many diverse people come to America? Look at a map of the continents. There are other places to go. There are riches and opportunity elsewhere. But our nation has had a special attraction for peoples from all over the world.

Do you want to meet someone from Itaituba? Or Narssarssuaq? Or Alma Ata? Try the United States; somewhere you'll find them.

Why did they come here? Why did most of us come here?

Is it because of the freedom that the United States offers? Yes, in great part it is.

But not everyone came for freedom: some came looking for gold, or other ways to get rich. They soon discovered that they also were enriched by America's freedom. Free nations are almost always more prosperous than enslaved nations. So many Americans did become rich. And, rich or poor, most came to love the ideas of freedom they found here. They especially loved that idea of religious freedom, because religious beliefs are our deepest beliefs. Religious freedom is the freedom to think for yourself: to have ideas, to have beliefs, to have a conscience. Religious freedom even gives you the right to reject all formal religions and not believe in a god.

We have that right in the United States. What has that done for us?

A Frenchman, whose name was Alexis de Tocqueville, came here in the 19th century and was astounded by much of what he saw:

"In France I had almost always seen the spirit of religion and the spirit of freedom pursuing courses diametrically opposed to each other; but in America I found that they were intimately united."

De Tocqueville was amazed: he found that the freedom not to be religious had made many of us religious! And while church attendance figures have changed over time, in 2015, Wikipedia said that, "A majority of Americans report that religion plays a very important role in their lives, a proportion unique among developed countries." How did that happen?

There is a shameful exception to the freedom story in America. While some Americans were demanding freedom from England and making sure their nation's founding documents provided for that freedom, they were enslaving workers. It was a horrendous error. It was an awful injustice. It was hypocritical. It is part of our history. Many of America's early settlers thought that history would ignore the nasty mistake they were making. But history doesn't forget. As for those who were enslaved: they and their descendants understood and cherished the power of freedom more than most Americans. In the 20th century, they would energize a Civil Rights movement that has inspired all Americans (and the rest of the world too).

3 Some History: American, European, and English

There were religions in the land before the newcomers arrived: Native American religions. The practices of those indigenous (it means native or original) religions varied: there were the gentle ceremonies of the islander Arawaks, the healing chants of the Navajo, the fierce rituals of the sacrifice-demanding Aztecs, and more. The American-born religions went from primitive to sophisticated, yet held a common thread: most found God in nature. Those Indian religions were shunted aside by the European invaders and became a sidebar in American history.

It was the European religions that came to dominate the nation-that-would-be. Thus, to understand the United States, and the beliefs that formed the nation, it helps to consider the European people—and their beliefs.

Most Europeans were Christians—and had been since about the Fourth Century. Christianity has two ancient branches: the oldest is called Eastern Orthodox and originated in the Middle East. The other is called Roman Catholic (its name tells you where it is centered).

In Christopher Columbus's day the Eastern (sometimes called Greek) Orthodox Church held sway in the Near East and Russia, but it was to the church in Rome that most Europeans offered allegiance. That was until Martin Luther, in 1517, nailed a list of grievances (complaints) on a church door in Wittenburg, Germany.

Luther was a Catholic priest and also a professor at Wittenburg University (where Shakespeare sent Hamlet to college). Luther didn't mean to start a religious revolution; he just wanted to reform the Roman Catholic Church. There were practices in the Church of his time that he thought were wrong. For instance: priests were selling what were called "indulgences" to people who had sinned. If they paid enough it was supposed to keep them from going to Hell. Luther spoke out strongly against that practice. He also

Martin Luther, painted by his friend Lucas Cranach the Elder

wrote that the Bible is the only source of divine knowledge, which challenged the authority of the Pope, the Bishops, and other Church officials. When Luther refused to retract his writings he was excommunicated (kicked out of the Church) by the Pope; at the same time, Europe's major political figure, the Holy Roman Emperor Charles V, called Luther an outlaw. But Luther's timing was propitious: there were many in Europe who were ready for change.

When he translated the Holy Bible into everyday German it made that work available to everyone who could read that language: his work would lead to translations of the Bible into other languages.

Luther's protests led to Protestantism (consider the root of that word) and a Christian tree full of branches. The new Protestant churches had varying ideas on worship, but all rejected the supremacy of the Roman pope. Most of the new churches reflected new beliefs or unhappiness with old beliefs, but in England the story was different. There the break with Rome came because King Henry VIII wanted to divorce his wife and the Pope said "no."

Henry got his way in 1534. That's when Parliament (England's Congress) established the Church of England, separating it from the Church in Rome, and making England's king its leader. Financially this turned out to be a good deal for England: Church money and power that had been going to Rome now stayed in Britain. Otherwise, the Church of England, which was also called the Anglican Church, kept most of the practices of the Roman Church.

There is still more to this. Most emperors and kings, including King Henry VIII, believed in "divine right," which means they said their leadership was sanctioned by both God and Church. Luther's action was also a threat to that idea. It was a big step toward separating Church and State.

It was also confusing. Some people wanted things to stay as they had been; some wanted change. Everyone was claiming to be doing God's will. On the European continent that confusion and turmoil led directly to the Thirty Years' War (1618-1648), which was all about religious differences (Protestants vs. Catholics) and turned out to be one of the bloodiest and most awful wars in all of world history. In the German city of Brandenburg, more than half the population died. When armies didn't kill, disease often did. Sometimes with an army on the way, everyone fled from their town, which meant they might soon be sleeping in the woods, and starving, or fighting off wild animals. Then crops failed. Why did all this happen? No one knew but it was easy to blame it on witches, so there was a whole lot of witch-hunting and hanging. It was a horrible time for most Europeans (some fled to America).

This work by Johann Jakob Wick shows a trio of accused witches meeting a terrible end

Things got further complicated in England—and bloody too—because King Henry VIII's oldest daughter, Mary, stayed Catholic.

(Known as Mary I or Mary Tudor, she had red hair, a pretty face, brains, and musical talent too.) When her father died, Mary's brother became King Edward IV, but soon died of illness. Mary became Queen of England and Ireland, and brought the Roman Catholic Church back to power. Some people were happy about that; others were enraged. Money and power changed hands again, and Mary burned more than 280 Protestants at the stake (that's why she is sometimes known as Bloody Mary). Mary married Philip of Spain; he imagined that the marriage would help create a great Catholic empire that stretched across Europe.

Then Mary died. Henry VIII had another daughter, Elizabeth: she was Protestant and next in line for the throne. When Elizabeth became Queen the English people must have felt as if they were riding on a tennis ball. Now they were back in the Church of England's court.

As it turned out, Queen Elizabeth's reign was a time of intellectual and cultural ferment that still leaves us awestruck almost five hundred years later. Those were the days of William Shakespeare, Sir Francis Bacon, John Donne (one of my favorite poets), and Sir Walter Raleigh. It was when Pocahontas visited England, caught smallpox, and died. It was when Dr. William Harvey figured out that blood circulates in the body and is not constantly being generated—as all the medical schools taught. It was when Robert Hooke looked through a microscope, focused on small bits of life, named tiny structures he saw "cells," and published a book of amazing pictures sharing what he had seen. A Dutchman who saw Hooke's book went further. He built a better viewing device, got some spittle from an old man's mouth, and was the first to see bacteria and other inhabitants of the microbial world (his name was Antonie van Leeuwenhoek).

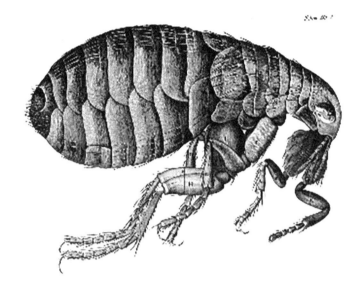

Hooke's famous flea

Exciting as these times seem to us looking backward, they seemed immoral and out-of-control to many—especially the pious—who were living through them.

Devout English Christians began protesting against what they believed was the laxness of the Church of England. They didn't think that King James I, who followed Queen Elizabeth in 1603, was leading the church as some said he should. (Think about politics today; people rarely agree about their leaders.) James I was called "the wisest fool in all of Christendom."

Actually he was a thoughtful, scholarly man who decided to commission a new translation of the Bible. He got a committee of religious scholars to do the work and they came up with an amazing document. Known as the King James Bible, it turned out to be a work of great eloquence that still impacts literary writing in the English language. (There are varying opinions on how good a biblical translation it is.)

James was not gifted when it came to political leadership. But on

King James I by John de Critz the Elder

one subject King James had no doubts: he was sure God made him king and meant for him to rule. As God's chief decision- maker he thought there was a limit on what he should allow in the way of dissent in England. So in 1620 when some bothersome zealots, the Pilgrims, decided to sail to the wilds of the new continent, James gladly waved them off.

They weren't the first English men and women to go to America. Explorer/navigator John Davys reached that unexplored continent in the 1580s in search of a river ships could use to sail across America. It was called the Northwest Passage and it didn't exist (it does now because of global warming), but no one knew that. Davys hoped America was just a slim strip of land. Looking west from Newfoundland he didn't know a huge continent stretched ahead.

Davys had another mission: to spread the gospel to the natives he encountered, so he had his sailors sing and dance to hymns. The Inuit didn't like his music. They stole his anchor. Here are some of Davys' words about what he saw as a godly task:

> "There is no doubt that we of England are this saved people, by the eternal and infallible presence of the Lord predestined to be sent into these Gentiles in the sea… there to preach to the people

of the Lord… to give light to all the rest of the
world… It is only we, therefore, that must be these
shining messengers of the Lord, and none but we."

"Only we?" "None but we?" How might other people react to that
idea?

A few years later, in 1607, a small group of Englishmen lands at
Jamestown (yes, the name honors King James I). They are more
interested in finding gold than in saving souls, although they
believe they can do both. They have sailed into a great natural
port (it will be called Hampton Roads) in Virginia (named for
virgin Queen Elizabeth). Jamestown is an island up the James
River. They don't know it, but there is no gold in Virginia.
Searching for it is hard work; so is raising crops and building
shelters in an unknown land filled with mosquitoes and germs for
which they have no immunity. The first years are horrendous for
this small colony. There are many deaths, although the settlers do
get some help from a young Indian princess named Pocahontas.
By 1618 and 1619 the worst is over and the colony seems to be
surviving. That's when London's Virginia Company sends 100 boys
and girls, ages 8 to 16, to Virginia to do whatever work needs
doing. These are children found begging on the streets of
London. Given the choice of jail or the colonies, some choose jail.

It is a very different story in 1620 when the Pilgrims decide to
head for Virginia. They are religious Separatists: they want to
separate themselves from the King's church and get as far from
England's politics as possible. They want to be somewhere they
can pray as they wish.

The Pilgrims have been to Holland to try and live a godly life.
Mostly they found was holy poverty. Life in the Netherlands wasn't
for them: their children were soon speaking Dutch, not English.

So in 1620, they head for a Hudson River site (then considered to be in Virginia). The ship's captain gets lost trying to find it and they end up in Massachusetts at a place they name Plymouth.
There they find land cleared and ready for planting, but no people are around. Smallpox caught from European fishermen has killed most of the native population. They see that as an omen from God.

Meanwhile, another group of deeply religious people, the Puritans, alarmed by corruption in England's church, decide to leave for what they call the "New World." They are not separatists. They want to be part of the King's Anglican Church, but they want to reform and purify it (and maybe play leadership roles). The King doesn't want to be reformed. Things get bad for the Puritans in England, so bad that they decide to follow the Pilgrims to Massachusetts (to live in different settlements). After they make that voyage, others, including some unusual religious thinkers called Quakers, also sail to the New World. And some Baptists do too.

It is those Pilgrims and Puritans (don't confuse them) and Quakers and Baptists who begin the story of religious freedom in America.

From our beginnings, we were a mélange, a mixture of thinking people. What happened to all those who were sure they knew God's truth? Keep reading for more of their story.

4 Baptists and Pilgrims: Think for Yourselfers

When Henry VIII split with the Catholic Church and made himself head of the Anglican Church, he didn't intend for much to get changed, except that church politics and funds were to stay in England.

Church services would remain the same, with only two differences: the worship of "idols" was forbidden (shrines would soon be destroyed throughout the realm) and—this is big—every church was to have a Bible, written in English and available for anyone to read.

Traditional Catholic services were in Latin. Catholic Bibles were also in Latin, which meant only the scholarly could read them. Now ordinary English men and women who attended Anglican services had a Holy Bible they could read themselves; they were able to consider what it said and draw their own conclusions. No one had thought about how revolutionary this would be; it led to unexpected outcomes. Suddenly a lot of people wanted to learn to read. Literacy boomed.

Something else: anyone who has studied the Bible will tell you that most of its passages can be interpreted in more than one way. Before, priests had preached an official version of scripture and their parishioners couldn't question them because they couldn't read the text themselves. Now they could. Some began asking questions, doing deep thinking, and disagreeing with priestly interpretations. Out of this ferment came some dissenting groups who wanted to break away from the Church of England. Those dissenters asked for what they said was freedom of conscience. What they meant was the freedom to interpret the Bible for themselves.

John Smyth and Thomas Helwys were two early questioners; they may have been the first to put their dissenting ideas into clear prose. Eventually they would become founders of the Baptist Church in England. Smyth wrote, "the magistrate is not by virtue of his office to meddle with religion, or matters of conscience." When he said "magistrate" he meant the king and his officers around the country. In other words: a king's power is over earthly affairs, but not over matters of belief or "conscience." In a world where the king's power was absolute, this was a new and dangerous thought.

To clarify: Smyth was saying that the domain and power of rulers belong in laws, but matters of conscience, or belief, are beyond a government's laws. They are inside heads and hearts and are private territory. The Baptists said religion is a personal affair between men and women and their God.

Now that was a world-shattering thought! If the king didn't tell you, how would you know what to think? Or so some people wondered. Some dissenters get burned at the stake in England. Some are thrown in jail. When Smyth, who had been an Anglican priest, begins preaching these new thoughts in the small city of Lincoln he is in trouble. Around 1602 he flees to Holland with some other dissenters. In The Netherlands Smyth studies the Bible intensely. Something doesn't make sense to him: infants (who can't think for themselves) are baptized into the Anglican Church. Smyth says it should be thinking, believing adults, not infants, who are baptized. But what if an unbaptized child dies? Will his soul go to heaven? This is a big issue: Smyth says "yes," others say "no."

In 1612 Smyth is back in England where he, Thomas Helwys, and a small group of followers found the first Baptist congregation.

That same year Helwys writes that the King of England can "command what of man he will, and we are to obey it," but as for religious belief, "with this Kingdom, our lord the King hath nothing to do." (Read that a few times to be sure you get it.) Helwys gets thrown in prison.

So does Leonard Busher, a follower of Helwys, who writes what is believed to be the earliest known treatise dealing exclusively with the subject of religious liberty. It is titled *Religious Peace; or, a Plea for Liberty of Conscience, long since presented to King James and the High Court of Parliament then sitting, by L. B., Citizen of London, and printed in the year 1614.*

Does King James I read it? Maybe. He is a reading, thinking man. Speaking to Parliament in 1614 he says, "No state can evidence that any religion or heresy was ever extirpated by the sword or by violence, nor have I ever judged it a way of planting the truth." (Can you write this in words that can be easily understood? Extirpated means removed or destroyed.)

Do King James I's thoughts make a difference? Not to Thomas Helwys, who dies in jail in 1616. No one is sure what happened to Leonard Busher. But we do know that a young man named Roger Williams reads Busher's document and later quotes some of its words. Roger Williams will sail for America (his story is coming) but not with the first English group that crosses the Atlantic seeking religious freedom.

They are dissenters and separatists who come from a small English town named Scrooby. Aware of the religious freedom

John Smyth found in the Netherlands, they too cross the North Sea where they find the freedom they seek, but Holland isn't England and they want to raise their children and pray to God in an English environment. They don't agree with Smyth and Helwys on that Baptism issue, and they are very aware of the fate of dissenters in England. So in 1620, 102 of them head for America on a small ship named the *Mayflower*. They call themselves "saints." Others will call them Pilgrims.

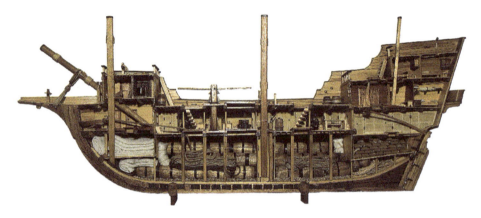

This model shows a cross-section of a 17th century merchant ship similar to the Mayflower. Close quarters for the Pilgrims!

As it happens, those who climb aboard the *Mayflower* have a history of goofing up. When they first leave England for Holland (which is illegal to do) they sell their homes and give money for the trip across the North Sea to a skipper who pockets the cash and turns them over to English authorities. With their money and homes gone they are in trouble. But finally they make it to Amsterdam and then the town of Leyden. There they have religious freedom but not much more. And they don't speak Dutch. So they decide to try life in what is being called "a New World."

As for the long trip across the Atlantic? Two ships, the *Mayflower* and the *Speedwell*, are supposed to make the voyage. The

Speedwell leaks, and the Pilgrims waste a month trying to deal with it; finally it is abandoned and the already crowded *Mayflower* gets even more crowded. Bathroom facilities consist of a bucket; everyone uses the same one, throwing its contents into the ocean.

LANDING OF THE PILGRIMS AT PLYMOUTH 11ᵗʰ DEC. 1820.

Here's how a 19th century artist pictured the Pilgrims' arrival in their new land

Sixty-six days after they set sail the Pilgrims land in a place they name Plymouth Bay. Their adventure is just getting started. These are village folks who must attempt to be hunter/gatherer/ planters on an unknown-to-them continent. A year later, half of the Pilgrims are dead, of starvation, disease, and the cold. Those who survive create the Plymouth Colony.

These Pilgrims are not to be confused with others known as Puritans, a much larger and better-supplied group who set sail a few years later. The Puritans don't want to leave the Anglican Church, as the Pilgrims do. The Puritans intend to purify that church by living and worshipping as they believe God wants them to live and worship. In England, given its politics and problems, they have been unable to do so.

Try Reading Words from the Past

Words from the past help you see events through the eyes of those who lived before us. They help you hear language of other times. Language and its rhythms change over time. That can make reading works from the past a challenge, like solving a puzzle. People who spoke English sounded different several hundred years ago. They used different phrases. So don't be discouraged if you find these documents difficult. They are. Just take them sentence-by-sentence and you will understand. Imagine that you are translating a foreign language; this one just happens to be an early version of English.

Another problem: many of the original words that come to us from history are legal documents. Then and now legal language is often written for other lawyers, not for laypeople. So take a deep breath and do your best to decipher it. Just think of it as a code and imagine that you are a code breaker.

Something to think about when you read an original document: people in the past, like people today, don't always tell the truth. Sometimes they make mistakes. So just because it is old doesn't mean it is true. Still, these documents can be links to others we wish we could have known.

From the Capital Laws of New Plymouth, 1636

(Not to be confused with New Plymouth in New Zealand, a 19th century British settlement).

It is Enacted by this Court, and the Authority thereof, That if any Person having had the knowledge of the true God, openly and manifestly, have or worship any other God but the Lord God, he shall be put to Death. Exodus.22.20, Deuteronomy. 13.6, 10.

2. If any Person within this Jurisdiction professing the True God, shall wittingly and willingly presume to Blaspheme the Holy Name of God the Father, Son, or Holy Ghost, with direct, express, presumptuous, high-handed Blasphemy, either by willful or obstinate denying of the true God or His Creation or Government of the World or shall curse God, Father, Son or Holy Ghost, such person shall be put to Death. Leviticus 24. 15, 16.

3. Treason against the Person of our Sovereign Lord the King, the Realm and Commonwealth of England, shall be punisht by Death.

4. That whosoever shall Conspire and Attempt any invasion, Insurrection, or public Rebellion against this Jurisdiction and his Majesties Authority here established, or surprize any Town, Plantation, Fortification or Ammunition therein provided for the safety thereof; or shall treacherously and perfidiously attempt and endeavor the Alteration and Subversion of our Fundamental Frame and Constitution of this Government, every such Person shall be put to death.

Key Phrase in this Document:

I think it is "put to death." See if you agree. Once you find a key phrase usually the rest of the document makes sense. When and why were people "put to death" in New Plymouth? Was New Plymouth a Pilgrim or Puritan settlement? Did that make a difference on this issue? Why did these thoughtful people believe that sometimes they needed to kill in the name of God? Are there people today killing in God's name?

Questions and Answers:

1. What are Exodus, Deuteronomy and Leviticus?
   They are books in the Hebrew Bible. If you want to go further, look them up.
2. What are capital crimes?
   They are crimes punished by death.
3. What do the first two laws deal with? The next two?
   The first deal with relations with God, specifically blasphemy. The next two deal with violations against state laws. What about death-penalty crimes today?
4. Are blasphemers killed in some nations today?
   Yes. In Iran, Saudi Arabia, and some other nations speaking out against religious belief is a capital crime, sometimes leading to beheading.

Suggestion:

Look up the cited Biblical passages. Comment on them in terms people in the 17th century might use, and then as you see them today. How do your responses differ?

Thinking as Historians:

To think as a historian you need to transport yourself back to the 17th century and see the capital laws of the Plymouth Colony in context. They were part of the "General Fundamentals" of the Plymouth Colony, a set of laws that seemed enlightened in their day. Most people agreed those laws were necessary; today we are horrified by some of them. Can we guess how people 400 years from now will feel about our ideas and practices? What about today's legal killings? What are they?

5 Setting Sail for Freedom

What gives the Puritans the courage to climb onto tiny wooden ships and brave a fierce ocean? They are leaving England with its great cathedrals and green hills and fine universities. They are leaving all they know and love, perhaps forever.

These Puritans are different from the Pilgrims who sailed on the rickety *Mayflower*. Those voyagers back in 1620 were mostly working class folk who rejected the ways of the established Church of England and set up their own church in Plymouth. The Pilgrims wanted no part of the Anglican Church practices.

The Puritans, who come a decade and more later, are members of the Anglican Church, but unhappy with what it has become. They are perfectionists and purists and they want their church to go farther than the King will take it. They want to get rid of some practices left over from Catholicism. They want to get rid of favoritism and corruption in the Church.

Their discontent is matched by that of a growing class of poor people now leaving rural areas for overcrowded cities. The King and his ministers don't seem to be dealing with the nation's problems. The Puritans, who want to focus on finding God's way, hope to create a perfect society, and faraway America seems one place to do it.

They are not n'er-do-wells, or paupers, or criminals (although plenty of those kinds will come to America). No, the Puritans are substantial people. Their leader, John Winthrop, leaves a manor when he heads to the wilds of America. Others leave farms and businesses. Theirs is a massive migration: perhaps 20,000 Puritans will come to New England between 1630 and 1650. Unlike most of the early migrants, they come with their families. It takes courage to be among them. What gives them that courage? They believe that they know God's truth.

John Winthrop preaches a famous sermon on board the ship *Arabella* on its way to America. He uses a phrase from Jesus's Sermon on the Mount, found at Matthew 5:14. Jesus tells his listeners, "You are the light of the world. A city that is set on a hill cannot be hidden." Winthrop believes that he and his fellow Puritans have entered into a covenant or contract with God. "For we must consider that we shall be as a City upon a Hill, the eyes of all people are upon us." Those heading for America are inspired by that idea.

To our eyes the reforming Puritans and the separatist Pilgrims don't seem very different. They both read the Hebrew Bible and the Christian Scriptures, also called the Old and New Testaments, and both take those texts very seriously. Each is convinced that his path to God is the only true one.

Both Pilgrims and Puritans follow the teachings of John Calvin, who believed that only a few people have been chosen by God to be saved and sent to heaven. Since God knows everything He knows who those "elect" few are. You are either among them, or you aren't. Nothing you can do will put you there. By searching their souls these dedicated believers hope to find clues as to whether they are among the elect. Puritans believe that God's elect are meant to rule and guide others.

Suppose someone doesn't want to accept guidance? Suppose

someone reads the Bible and interprets it for himself (or herself)?
Well, the Puritans don't want anyone like that in their community.
One of their governors, Thomas Dudley, writes:

> Let men and God in courts and churches watch
> O'er such as do a toleration hatch. . .

In other words, watch out for those who promote toleration. For
Puritans, toleration means allowing people to believe wrong
thoughts. They have come too far and suffered too many
hardships to allow that.

So was it religious freedom that made them cross an ocean? Yes
and no. They want religious freedom for themselves, but not for
others who worship differently. They believe there is only one true
path to God and that they are on it. This is not religious freedom
as we now know it. Roger Williams—who you'll soon read
about—will define religious freedom as freedom of conscience:
the freedom to be true to your own beliefs, whatever they are,
which is what most of us seek today.

Thomas Jefferson—who lived more than a hundred years after
Roger Williams—will go even farther when he says your religious
beliefs are no one's business but your own. Each of us has a right
to choose a religion, or no religion, and that right is a natural
right, beyond the power of governments.

That is what Thomas Jefferson told us, and today most of us
believe it is so. The Puritans would have thought us all crazy, and
sinful too. They would have locked Jefferson in jail. They kicked
Roger Williams out of their colony. Couldn't they understand that
each of us has the right to our own beliefs?

No, they couldn't. And chances are most of us wouldn't have
understood it either, had we lived in their times. That very simple

Puritans as Slaveowners

This is a difficult subject. Some Puritans own slaves. Some make money on the slave trade. They are doing what a lot of other people do, especially the rich and powerful. Have you ever used the phrase, "everyone else does it" as an excuse? In early America, owning slaves usually meant being rich; not owning slaves often meant being poor. If you lived in a slaveowning family in the 17th century, you would probably die still owning slaves. In most Southern colonies you needed slaves if you wanted to be prosperous.

A few people didn't go along with the crowd. A few people, very few, freed their slaves. What gives some people the courage to do the right thing? See what you can find out about John Newton, who wrote the song, "Amazing Grace." Read about William Wilberforce. Then read about David George and Lemuel Haynes: both were black preachers (there's a chapter on Haynes later in this book).

idea—that we have a right to the freedom of our minds—is surprisingly sophisticated. It took centuries to evolve. It is America's most profound contribution to political theory. It is a freedom that is still not granted in many of the world's nations.

The first English settlers were searching, honestly searching, for "the" truth. The problem in the English colonies was that Puritans saw one truth, Church of England members another, Catholics another, and Baptists and Methodists yet another. Since each believed his was the only true path, each saw it as a duty to make all others walk the same path. How do you do that? You can try persuasion. If that doesn't work, you may be forced to try torture, or hanging.

Take yourself to Boston in 1651, some thirty years after the *Mayflower*'s arrival, and you'll see a Baptist being lashed on his bare back for daring to enter Massachusetts territory. To Boston's true believing Puritans, Baptist beliefs are heresy. They think they are doing God's will by beating him.

And then there are the Quakers, a sect of separatists with ideas about peace and equality that, in the 17th century, seem very strange indeed.

So when Quakers come to New England the Puritans whip them and send them away. But the Quakers are intense believers: they want to pursade others and also save their own souls. So they come back, again and again. Finally there seems nothing to do but hang them. The Puritans don't understand: you can't force faith. We know that; that's why we believe in religious freedom. But a few Puritans are beginning to question the orthodox Puritan vision. John Winthrop, Jr., who was governor of Connecticut, and son of the Massachusetts governor, pleads "as on his bare knees" that the Quakers not be hanged. It does no good. For those who are true believers the Quakers have to go.

A modern Christian rapper, Propaganda, has written a song titled "Precious Puritans." The lyrics include this line: "your precious Puritans' partners purchased people." Then Propaganda goes on, realizing we all do things that are not right, and asks, "Are you inerrant?" ("Inerrant" means incapable of mistakes, or without error.)

6 A Man With 'Newe and Dangerous Ideas'

How do we deal with prayer in schools where Muslims sit next to Methodists and Catholics eat lunch with Jews? We live in pluralistic times, yet our differences can still pose a challenge. Dealing with differences was a terrible challenge for the Puritans.

How were the Massachusetts Puritans to handle Roger Williams: a man whose intellect and piety were stunning but whose thoughts led him in directions that seemed to threaten the Puritan way?

The answer was not easy. The Puritans of the Massachusetts Bay Colony discoursed long and thoughtfully, for they knew this was a question that tested their deepest convictions. The answer they came to was banishment. To protect that which they thought most precious—their faith—they believed they must exile those who differed.

It didn't help. Sheep may all bray to the same tune (and even that is unlikely) but people don't all believe alike. At least thinking people don't. And so the Puritans often drove away their brightest: those who asked the most questions.

The most devoted of them all may have been Roger Williams. Many Puritans thought so, which made it a wrenching decision to cast him out from Massachusetts, especially for the governor, the good and reasonable John Winthrop.

Roger Williams would have had trouble fitting in any time or place. He was, as they say, too good to be true. He had that rare ability to see that the Emperor is without clothes, and the even rarer courage to say so. And that was only part of what made him disturbing to others.

Roger Williams

Williams was a Puritan (at least he began that way), but his views soon led him to Separatist and then Baptist and then Independent ways. He could not tolerate what he saw as the corruption of the English (Anglican) Church, so he came to Massachusetts. He was brilliant, and thoughtful, and kind, and had all the charismatic qualities that draw people to a natural leader. And he was intensely devout.

He was mentored, as a young man, by Sir Edward Coke (pronounced like cook), who was the most renowned jurist of his time and an expert on England's common law. Common law is built on previous legal decisions. There is no written constitution (as we have in the United States). In Coke's day the king often claimed divine right. In other words he said because he was king he had the right to do whatever he wanted. Jurists like Coke said the king had to obey the common law. In the United Kingdom (Scotland and England) today, most law is influenced by Coke's thinking and based on common law.

Roger Williams' reputation as a deeply religious, thinking man preceded him to New England; when he arrived he was asked to be teacher and minister at the church in Boston. It was the best job he could have been offered. But he turned it down. The ways of the congregation were not sufficiently pure for him.

Should Writers Be Free to Write What They Want? What About Censors? What About Separation of Church and State?

John Milton (1608-1674) was the most famous English writer of his time (he lived in the generation after William Shakespeare). Milton and Roger Williams (1603-1683) were good friends when both were students at Cambridge University. Milton tutored Williams in Hebrew (so he could read the Old Testament in its original language) and Williams tutored Milton in Dutch (Holland was becoming a powerhouse nation). Even today, Milton's poem *Paradise Lost* is read by just about everyone who cares about English literature. It is still considered one of the greatest poems in the English language.

Milton also wrote about political issues. In *Areopagitica*, a published paper addressed to "the Parliament of England," he argued for freedom of speech and freedom of the press. "Give me the liberty to know, to utter and to argue freely according to conscience, above all liberties," he wrote. Milton also made a case for disestablishment. That means he wanted the Church to be separate from the British government. Milton believed the gospel could persuade on its own; it shouldn't need government backing.

If you visit the main reading room at the New York Public Library, look up. This quotation from *Areopagitica* is over the entrance: "A good book is the precious lifeblood of a master spirit, embalmed and treasured up on purpose to a life beyond life."

So off he went to Salem where people were more separatist in their outlook. There the intensity of his beliefs began to lead him—one step at a time—into a relationship with God that he could share with no one.

It was logical that he would get there. Wanting extreme purity, he began discarding the layers of human activities that stood between him and his God. This took him to a kind of personal theology that he couldn't share easily; it also led him to understand that others might have beliefs that were different from his but appropriate for them. Williams' intellectual honesty forced him to ask questions: Is it possible that there can be more than one path to God? Or, if there is only one path, how can any human be sure he is on it? And can it be right to kill in the name of God?

Some of his questions threatened the Puritan church in America. How, he asked, could the king charter and sell land that did not belong to him? Shouldn't the Indians be paid for their land?

Now that was an unacceptable question. He was questioning the king and the whole English concept of rights and power. No matter that Roger Williams' question was logical, and ethical too; if the king heard that question he might just revoke the charter of the Massachusetts Bay Colony and order everyone home.

So there seemed no way around it. This kind, lovable, pious man was dangerous. He was found guilty of holding "newe & dangerous ideas." The decision of the Puritan court was to ship him back to England.

When Roger Williams' wife heard the news she cried. Williams consoled her, saying, "Fifty good men did what they thought was just." Williams was even able to look at his accusers with fairness.

But he wasn't about to go back to England, so he ran off, to the wilds of Rhode Island in the fierceness of a January snow. The Narragansett Indians, who were said to be heathens, gave him shelter. Williams learned to love and respect them as they would love and respect him.

It was in Rhode Island, at a place he named Providence, that his ideas evolved into a practical means of governing. Roger Williams found a way for people with deeply different ideas to live together. He did that by establishing a governing body that did not meddle with affairs of faith. The Rhode Island charter said no one should be "in any wise molested, punished, disquieted, or called in question for a difference in opinion in matters of religion." In other words, governments should stick to civil matters. We call that separation of church and state. It was an untried idea. Throughout history, Kings had claimed "divine right," which they said meant God approved of their reign. Most political leaders went along with that belief, because it helped give them power too. Since most people couldn't read, and those who did rarely saw newspapers (and this was way, way before television), it was easy to believe whatever you were told.

 In the best circumstances, religious dissenters were tolerated. In the worst, they were killed. Roger Williams questioned all that: he established the first political entity, anywhere that we know about, founded on ideas of religious liberty and separation of church and state. And it worked. Outcasts, weirdos, and the intensely pious all came to Rhode Island—often because they were not wanted elsewhere—and they lived together with a measure of respect and harmony. They didn't change each other's views. They learned to live with their differences. They must have surprised themselves.

Even Roger Williams, with his innate graciousness, was amazed that those whose philosophy he abhorred—like Quakers and

Catholics and atheists—could be decent people. Dealing with Native Americans, and finding friends among them, he asked, "Whence cometh the morality of the atheist?" Others of his time never even asked.

Note

In 1644 Roger Williams published a defense of religious freedom called *The Bloody Tenet of Persecution for the Cause of Conscience Discussed.* (Tenet means belief or theory.)

Here are some words from *The Bloody Tenet*:

"…all men may walk as their consciences persuade them, every one in the name of his God. And let the saints of the Most High walk in this colony without molestation…"

("Without molestation" means without being arrested or attacked.)

Roger Williams, On the Limits of Freedom, 1655

Can you have freedom and an orderly society? That question obsessed people in the 17th century; it still troubles us today. In the 17th century most people thought you had to belong to a church in order to know how to behave. They thought that one of the roles of government was to make you go to church. People like the Puritans were sure that religious freedom would lead to both anarchy and immorality.

But Roger Williams began to think about the way people behave and why, and soon he believed differently. He thought that religion—and its formal structures of minister and church—should have one jurisdiction and that civil government—and its formal structures of lawmakers and governor—should have another.

Let's let Roger Williams speak for himself. He wrote these words in 1655:

There goes many a ship to sea, with many hundred souls in one ship, whose weal or woe is common, and is a true picture of a commonwealth, or a human combination or society. It hath fallen out sometimes, that both papists and protestants, Jews and Turks, may be embarked in one ship; upon which supposal I affirm, that all the liberty of conscience, that ever I pleaded for, turns upon these two hinges—that none of the papists, protestants, Jews, or Turks, be forced to come to the ship's prayers or worships, nor compelled from their own particular prayers or worship, if they practice any. I further add, that I never denied, that notwithstanding this liberty, the commander of this ship ought to command the ship's course, yea, and also command that justice, peace and sobriety, be kept and practiced, both among the seamen and all the passengers. If any of the seamen refuse to perform their services, or passengers to pay their freight; if any refuse to help, in person or purse, toward the common charges or defense; if any refuse to obey the common laws and orders of the ship, concerning their common peace or preservation; if any shall mutiny and rise up against their commanders and officer; if any should preach or write that there ought to be no commanders or officers, because all are equal in Christ, therefore no masters nor officers, no laws nor orders, nor corrections nor punishments; —I say, I never denied, but in such cases, whatever is pretended, the commander or commanders may judge, resist, compel and punish such transgressors, according to their deserts and merits. This if seriously and honestly minded, may, if it so please the Father of Lights, let in some light to such as willingly shut not their eyes.

A Reading Tip:

When you read material from another age, or anything difficult, it helps to put it into your own words. Then look for some central thoughts and highlight them. Ask yourself these questions: Why am I reading this document? What do I expect it to tell me?

If you really want to understand it, read it through quickly for an overview, then reread and write it in your own words, then read it once more for final comprehension. Do that and you should pass any test with high grades! Remember: reading old documents isn't easy. People expressed themselves differently in the past than they do today. I think this document is amazing because of when it was written and the idea it carries. Do you agree?

Questions:

Answer with complete sentences.

1. Can you be completely free and live in a society with laws? Why? Why not?

2. What is Roger Williams saying about the separation of church and state in *On the Limits of Freedom?* Use some of his words when you answer the question.

3. Does Williams believe there should be civil authorities? Give reasons for your answer.

4. Roger Williams uses a metaphor in this selection. What is a metaphor? What is the one he uses? Hint: check the first sentence.

Note:

When Williams, or others of his time, use the word "papist" they mean Catholic. Catholics were unpopular in 17th century England and were persecuted and feared. Catholics were treated very differently in different periods of English history; those differences might be a good subject for a term paper. What about Catholics in Ireland? That's a really big story.

7 Statues on the Commons

The Puritans were dissenters in England. Some of them went right on dissenting when they reached their new home in America. This was a big problem in a colony where people took their beliefs very seriously.

So when Roger Williams challenged John Winthrop and the Massachusetts Bay Puritans the issue was not personal. It was more important than that. It was about that ever-present conflict between those with authority and those who disagree with them. **The Puritans had come to America in good part because they didn't agree with England's King and Parliament on what they saw as very important issues. Now the same conflict was arising in their Massachusetts colony. Can independent thought be allowed? That has been an issue since the very start of humanity.**

When Anne Hutchinson and Mary Dyer voiced ideas outside the mainstream, they added another dimension—female—to the pot. Hutchinson was intensely devout and very smart. She had deep concerns about some ideas within Puritan belief. She claimed to be directed by God through visions. People listened to her. Soon a group of people were following her and questioning the Puritan ministers who were running the colony. It was a theocracy: a government ruled in the name of God. What were those ministers to do? They tried Hutchinson in the Puritan court.

Read the record of that trial and you can't help but be impressed by Anne Hutchinson. She outwitted her accusers.

No question about it: she was brilliant. She was also a fanatic and convinced that she was speaking God's words. Her followers believed she was too. Governor Winthrop understood that. The question remains: can authority allow dissent? The Puritan leaders didn't think they could. And they had power. So Anne Hutchinson was banished from Massachusetts for "the danger of her course amongst us." She went to Rhode Island and started her own colony. Later she moved to New York where she was killed in an Indian attack. Governor Winthrop saw it as God's justice.

Mary Dyer, too, was Puritan and pious. Winthrop called Dyer a "very proper and fair woman." That was when he first knew her. She became a best friend to Anne Hutchinson. So when Hutchinson was cast out of Massachusetts, Mary Dyer, her husband William Dyer, and other believers went with her to Rhode Island.

Then Mary Dyer took a trip back to England and found other truths for herself. She became a member of the Society of Friends, the people known as Quakers. The Friends wanted to do more than purify the Church of England; they wanted to form a separate church. Each of us, said the Quakers, has an "inner light" with which we can find God on our own. If a person has his own inner light then he (or she) can be his own minister.

And so the Quakers believe. **In a Quaker meeting anyone may speak out; there are no ministers.** This egalitarian way of thinking was a huge challenge to authority at a time when equality seemed a dangerous idea. Oaths of loyalty to country and king were expected in England and just about everywhere

QUAAKERS VERGADERING.   FRONTI NULLA FIDES.   THE QUAKERS MEETING

This satirical print from around 1675 shows the disdain many felt towards Quakers and women preachers. Look at the dog peeing on the skirt of the woman at the right. What is the artist trying to say?

in the 17th century. Quakers refused to swear oaths of allegiance to anyone but God.

Church and the government were all part of one package in the old world. The church gave the king his "divine right" to govern. In return, the government gave the church support and land. That was the way it had always been. Now, people like the Quakers seemed to want to mess up tradition. If each person has his own divine inner light and can think for himself, why, the next step is to say he doesn't need a king or a state church. And Quakers did say something like that when they sat in their meetings. (A Quaker church service is called a "meeting.")

Mary Dyer is led to her execution in this work by an unknown 19th century artist

Quakers do not believe in baptism, formal prayer, or ordained ministers. They refuse to fight in wars. Women are treated as equals in spiritual matters. Quakers believe that freedom of conscience is a human right, not something a state gives to its citizens. They believe that church and state should be separate. In the 17th century most people saw this as dangerous thinking.

So maybe you can see why Quakers were hated and persecuted by the authorities in England. They weren't liked any better in the colonies. The magistrates of the Massachusetts Bay Colony called them the "cursed sect" and passed harsh laws to keep them away. Quakers came anyway; they were jailed, or "severly whipt," or fined, or branded, or sent back to England. That didn't stop them. Some Quakers, like Mary Dyer, seemed determined to be martyrs. When she came to Boston she was sent away. She came back. She was tried with two Quaker men; all were convicted and led to the gallows.

The men were hanged, but at the last minute Dyer was put on a horse and sent off to Rhode Island. She came back. Now what do you do with such a woman? A woman who cares so much about her religion that she will risk death to preach its message? You'd think the Puritans would have understood that. Maybe they did, and that's what scared them.

Most Puritans thought they had done everything they could to be fair to Mary Dyer. Remember it was a different world then—a medieval world. When people started talking of toleration, the Puritans "could hardly understand what was happening in the world," writes Perry Miller, a historian of the Puritans. For more from Perry MIller, read Chapter 23.

Civil War in England: Divine Right Loses

Even though settlers came from many different countries, the 13 original colonies were all under British rule. So when England had a Civil War (1642 to 1651) the American colonists paid attention. In brief, this is what happened: King Charles I's supporters (the Royalist Cavaliers) battled a group in Parliament led by Puritans and Oliver Cromwell (called Roundheads). Scotland and Ireland and Wales as well as England got involved. When the fighting was over, the Puritans and Cromwell had won. Charles I lost his head.

After that it was clear: no British monarch could govern without Parliament agreeing to his or her decrees. That concept got legally nailed a bit later in what was called the Glorious Revolution in 1668.

When the Puritans took the reins in Great Britain they changed. They had to. Instead of leading a small devout group of followers, the Puritans had to lead a diverse nation. The Puritans in America never went through that change process. Many stayed stuck in the early 17th century while the rest of the world moved on.

Mary Dyer in the Words of a Court in Her Time

From: Massachusetts Court Records, 1660, part 1:419.

The Second Sentence of Mary Dyer:

The whole Court mett together sent for Mary Dyer, who rebelliously, after sentence of death past against hir, returned into this jurisdiction. Being come before the Court, she acknowledged hirself to be Mary Dyer, the person, & was condemned by this Court to death. Being asked what she had to say why the sentence should not be executed, she gave no other answr but that she denied our lawe, came to beare witnes against it, & could not choose but come & doe as formerly. The whole Court mett together voted, that the said Mary Dyer, for hir rebelliously returning into this jurisdiction (notwithstanding the favor of this Court towards hir,) shall be, by the marshall generall, on the first day of June, about nine of the clocke in the morning, carried to the place of execution, and according to the sentence of the Generall Court in October last, be put to death; that the secretary issue out warrant accordingly; which sentence the Governor declared to hir in open Court; & warrant issued out accordingly to Edward Michelson, marshall generall, & to Captain James Oliver, & his order, as formerly.

Note: this is 17th century spelling. Don't try it at school unless you want a poor grade! The big idea here is that a court is deciding to kill a person for not agreeing with their society's ideas on religious belief. How do you think they justified that? Five hundred years from now, when people look back at our time, what do you think might cause them to ask, "But why?"

Topics for Class Discussion:

The Puritans had suffered persecution themselves, but they didn't seem to understand the golden rule (do unto others as you would have others do unto you.) Why? (This is a tough question.) Can you relate their insensitivity to any situation you have faced or know about?

In 1989, a Muslim leader, the Ayatollah Ruhollah Khomeini, called for the death of author Salman Rushdie. Rushdie's book, *The Satanic Verses*, was denounced as blasphemous (What does that mean?). Compare the actions of the Puritans with those of the Ayatollah.

Imagine that you are a judge on the court that tried Mary Dyer. Remember you are a Puritan and you have come across the ocean to be free to practice your beliefs without interference. You and your fellow Puritans are trying to build a perfect godly society: you call it "A City on A Hill." You expect it to change world history. You expect it to save people's souls. How do you feel about Mary Dyer?

What do you think about the statues of Dyer and Hutchinson in Boston today? Were those women heroic? Or were they just pests? What makes a hero? When we look at the past, where do we often find heroes? What does Dyer's story tell you about some believing people today? Do you think some of today's villains may be tomorrow's heroes? What kinds of clues can we look for in judging people?

Current Events:

Research religious extremism today: what about beheadings by religious extremists in the Middle East today? What is ISIS?

Part II

Why Be Tolerant?

Because we believe it is right to do so?
Because it makes practical sense?
What about that word: tolerate?

None of the English colonies had what we think of as religious freedom. Nowhere on Earth was there a government that offered it. Rulers were expected to tell their subjects what and how to believe. That was the way it had always been done. Those who didn't believe, or pretend to believe, could end up in jail, or worse.

Rhode Island was the exception, but it was a tiny colony and mocked by most of the others. Rogues' Island was what they called it, although those who visited often remarked on its prosperity and independence.

The really important colonies, like Massachusetts and Virginia, had government-established churches—Puritan in the North and Anglican in the South—and laws on the books that called heresy a capital crime and also made it a crime not to attend church services. Yet, despite those laws, breezes of religious tolerance were blowing in the American air. Europe's long and bloody religious war (the Thirty Years' War from 1618 to 1648), with Protestants killing Catholics and vice versa, had made some people question the intolerance of most religions of the day. **The American colonies, from their beginnings, became a haven for religious freethinkers. The land itself was so vast that**

outcasts could always find places beyond persecution.

North Carolina was such a place. Baptists, and others who were jailed in aristocratic Virginia, were usually left alone in its rolling foothills.

South Carolina had a charter that the liberal English philosopher, John Locke, is said to have helped write. In its original form, "Jews, heathens and dissenters" were granted equality. (Indians and blacks were not.) The Jews and heathens were left out of the final draft, but in practice, South Carolina, where the Anglican Church was established, was tolerant. Huguenots (French Protestants), persecuted in Europe because of their religion, came in substantial numbers to the Carolinas. South Carolina was lucky; those Huguenots were industrious settlers.

There was something else in America that led to tolerance. It was the pragmatism (the sensible practicality) that developed quickly in a country where all hands were needed for the enormous tasks of clearing and planting and building. Bigotry has a hard time where people are in short supply.

That was the problem Peter Stuyvesant faced when he tried to use his Old World goggles in America. Stuyvesant, who was governor of New Netherland for almost 20 years (beginning in 1647), was a member of the Dutch Reformed Church. If the Dutch Reformed Church was good enough for him, it should be good enough for anyone, or so he believed. But what should he do with people who didn't agree?

Stuyvesant's bosses back in Holland were practical businessmen who, more than anything, wanted their colony, New Netherland, to make a profit. They didn't care what religion the colonists followed; all that mattered was their willingness to work hard. And they were the bosses. So they forced tolerance on Governor Stuyvesant.

Another kind of practicality brought a measure of religious freedom to Maryland. The Catholic proprietor had to get along with the dominant Protestant sects: his was an underdog religion and outnumbered.

New Jersey got a charter—a fine charter—that allowed for some religious freedom. That was because the owners of the colony were willing to experiment. Those proprietors (Sir George Carteret and Lord John Berkeley) were thinking men and, like many in Europe, sick of religious wars and fighting. They listened to John Locke (who talked of tolerance) and the Quakers (who talked of love.) What happened in New Jersey? It opened its doors to people from Finland, England, Germany, Sweden and many other places. And they all managed to live together without killing each other.

Quaker idealism and kindness brought tolerance in Pennsylvania too. Perched right in the middle between Puritan Massachusetts and Anglican Virginia, Pennsylvania welcomed almost anyone who wished to come. When they arrived they found they could worship, or not worship, as they desired. What happened with no government authorities ordering citizens to church? Why, the colony prospered, that's what happened, and a surprising number of people went to church too.

A Letter to the Native Americans of Pennsylvania

October 18, 1681

My Freinds,

There is one great God and Power that hath made ye world and all things therein, so whom you and I and all People owe their being and wellbeing, and to whom you and I must one Day give an account, for all that we do in this world: this great Power God hath written his law in our hearts, by which we are taught and commanded to love and help and do good to one another, and not to do harme and mischeif unto one an'other. Now this great God hath been pleased to make me concerned in parts of the world, and the king of the Countrey where I live, hath given unto me a great Province therein, but I desire to enjoy it with your Love and Consent, that we may al – always live together as Neighbors and freinds, else what would the great God say to us, who hath made us not to devour and destroy one an other but live Soberly and kindly together in the world. Now I would have you well to observe, that I am very Sensible of the unkindness and Injustice that hath been too much exersised towards you by the People of thes Parts of the world, who have sought themselves, and to make great Advantages by you, rather then be examples of Good & Goodness unto you, which I hear, hath been matter of Trouble to you, and caused great Grudgings and Animosities, Sometimes to the Shedding of blood, which hath made the great God Angry. but I am not such a man, as is well known in my own Country: I have great love and regard towards you, and I desire to win and gain your Love & freindship by a kind, just and peaceable life; and the People I send are of the same mind, & Shall in all things behave themselvs accordingly; and if in any thing any Shall offend you or your People, you shall have a full and speedy Satisfaction for the same ^by an equal number on both sides that by no means you may have just occasion of being offended against them; I Shall Shortly come to you my Selfe. At what time we may more largely and freely confer discourse of thes matters; in the mean time I have sent my commissioners to you about to a league of the peace, left We desire you to be kind to my them people, and receive thes Presents and Tokens which I have sent to you, as a Testimony of my Good will to you, and my resolution to live Justly peaceably and freindy with you, I am your Freind.

WILLIAM PENN

8 Jews in New Amsterdam

Myth has it that the people of today's Belgium and Holland were fighting for religious freedom when they ousted Spain from what had been the Spanish Netherlands. That's a stretch, but it is certainly part of it. The Dutch were fighting for freedom from Spain's heavy-handed bureaucracy and from the Church's Inquisition, a court that terrorized and killed those who chose not to go along with the narrow interpretation of Catholicism followed by Spain's Philip II. That ruler didn't want Protestants, Jews, or Muslims in the lands he led and he made their lives impossible. Since there were a lot of Protestants in the Netherlands, that led to a rebellion. Philip II sent an army to fight the Protestants. England's Queen Elizabeth sent troops to help them. (The details on all this are interesting if you want to do some research.)

Some of the Netherlands' southern provinces stayed Catholic. They avoided the horrendous Thirty Years War (1618-1648) that would leave much of nearby Germany in ruins.

A conglomeration of Dutch city-states came out of all this; their leaders were more interested in encouraging business than involving themselves in the wars between Protestants and Catholics. The religious tolerance that emerged brought a variety of people to the Netherlands; it also brought new ideas, prosperity and eventually world power. (Remember, the Puritans went to Holland first, before climbing aboard the *Mayflower*). **The Netherlands transitioned from being a possession of the**

Holy Roman Empire (in the 1590s) to the greatest naval and economic power in the world (in the 17th century).

This led to a Dutch Golden Age. Skilled workers flocked to Holland, windmills and peat provided a source of power, business leaders invented modern financial methods, Dutch ships sailed to Japan and other Asian lands to trade, and great artists, like Rembrandt, found patrons.

The Dutch East India Company became the world's first multi-national corporation. But when the East India Company chose a governor for their small settlement on the North American mainland, it picked a bigot.

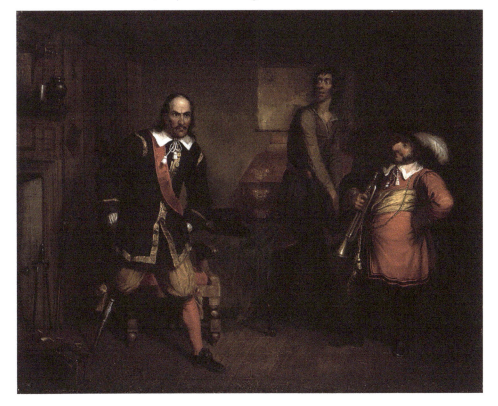

Would you have wanted to deliver bad news to Peter Stuyvesant? Here he reacts to word that a Dutch fort had fallen to the British..

There may not have been many candidates for the job. New Netherland was a wilderness post. Peter Stuyvesant, who was named governor, was an able administrator. He was also a tough, hard-swearing man who brooked no criticism. When his councilors made some suggestions he didn't like, he stomped on his wooden leg and told them he would ship them all back to Holland—cut up in pieces. When there were protests he loftily proclaimed that his authority came "from God and the Company, not from a few ignorant subjects."

So when a French ship pulled into New Amsterdam's magnificent harbor in 1654, with a few destitute Jews rescued from a pirate ship, Stuyvesant ordered them away. **The Jews, who were tough too, wouldn't go.** Stuyvesant sent a letter to his bosses in the Dutch East India Company asking for guidance. If he allowed them to stay, he wrote, why, he'd have to let in Lutherans and Papists (Catholics) too.

The Jews had come from Recife, in Brazil, where several thousand of them had lived in a prosperous colony. But, in a sense, their journey had begun more than a century earlier. It was on August 2, 1492—the very day that Columbus sailed from Palos—that all of Spain's Jews and Muslims were forced to leave the country. Jews had lived in Spain for 1,500 years. The Moors, or Muslims, had conquered the whole Iberian peninsula (Spain and Portugal) by 711. Muslims working together with Jews had helped create a golden—and tolerant—age in Spain. Scholarship and the arts had bloomed, and Muslims, Christians, and Jews alike had all prospered.

That didn't last long. There was soon warfare between Christians and Muslims (the Jews didn't have the power to make war). When Queen Isabella of Castile married Ferdinand II of Aragon they brought their kingdoms together and began the unification of

Spain. By the end of the 15th century Christian armies had won and most of Spain and Portugal were under Christian rule. In 1492, all Muslims and Jews were told they had to convert to Christianity or leave Spain. The converts needed to show that their conversion was sincere. If it wasn't—and sometimes torture helped "prove" their infidelity—they were burned at the stake. The Inquisition was the court that made decisions; the Inquisition's flames soon spread to other parts of Europe and finally to the New World.

So you can understand why Jews were among the first settlers in the Americas. They soon became prosperous planters and merchants, but by the middle of the 17th century the Inquisition had come to the New World. The Jews, who thought they had found a safe place to live, were again forced to flee, this time from South and Central America. Holland was one of the few places where they were welcome.

Sixteen ships set out from Recife for the Netherlands; one ship was captured by pirates. Then a French ship seized the pirate ship. Twenty-three Jews, whose possessions had all been taken, were hauled onto the French ship, which was headed for New Amsterdam. Now Peter Stuyvesant, who thought the Dutch Reformed Church was the only worthwhile church, had a problem. He wanted the Jews to leave. That's why he wrote a letter to the burghers back in Holland who ran the Dutch East India Company.

They saw things differently. Let the Jews stay, pay taxes, and worship privately, they said. But Peter Stuyvesant was right about something. There were soon Lutherans and Catholics in New Netherland, along with a whole polyglot population. In 1664, when the English took over New Amsterdam and named it New York, you could hear eighteen different languages being spoken on its streets. By this time the Jews had protested when they weren't allowed to do guard duty on the wall that enclosed the city. They wanted to be full citizens and do their civic duties. They got their way again, and were soon taking their turn doing that burdensome job. By the way, is New York still a polyglot city?

New Amsterdam Turns to New York

The colony dated its origin to 1609 when Henry Hudson (an Englishman working for the Dutch East India Company) charted all or parts of five future states: New York, New Jersey, Connecticut, Pennsylvania, and Delaware. A natural port, New Amsterdam, sat at the mouth of the Hudson River on Manhattan Island. Furs were soon traveling down the river and then were placed on ships bound for Europe.

When Peter Stuyvesant took charge, in 1647, there were about 500 colonists. The colony was constantly threatened: either by Native Americans or British marauders. Stuyvesant built a protective wall and the street next to it got called Wall Street; a nearby road was named Broadway.

In 1664, John Winthrop, Connecticut's governor, arrived in a small rowboat flying a white flag. He had an ultimatum from the King of England. Charles II had decided he wanted to take New Amsterdam and give it to his brother, the Duke of York. He sent a flotilla of four ships and 2,000 men to make it happen. Feisty Peter Stuyvesant wanted to resist. But the people of the colony didn't. New Amsterdam became New York. Stuyvesant and his council insisted in the Articles of Transfer that citizens "shall keep and enjoy the liberty of their consciences in religion." Stuyvesant seems to have learned something about the power of religious freedom, or maybe he was worried about his own religion. In either case, New York kept its tolerant ways.

Andrew Burnaby's Journal

New York, 1759

(This descriptive piece was written a century after Stuyvesant's time as mayor. The small island is Manhattan Island.)

The city is situated upon the point of a small island, lying open to the bay on one side, and on the others included between the North and East Rivers; and commands a fine prospect of water, the Jerseys, Long Island, Staten Island, and several others, which lie scattered in the bay. It contains between two and three thousand houses, and 16 or 17,000 inhabitants, is tolerably well built and has several good houses. The streets are paved, and very clean, but in general they are narrow; there are two or three, indeed, which are spacious and airy, particularly the Broad-Way. . .The whole length of the town is something more than a mile. . .The college, when finished, will be exceedingly handsome; it is to be built on three sides of a quadrangle, fronting Hudson's or North River, and will be the most beautifully situated of any college, I believe, in the world. . . The name of it is King's College.[1]

There are two churches in New York, the old or Trinity church, and the new one, or St. George's Chapel; both of them large buildings, the former in the Gothic taste, with a spire, the other upon the model of some of the new churches in London.[2] Besides these, there are several other places of religious worship; namely, two Low Dutch Calvinist churches, one High Dutch ditto, one French ditto, one German Lutheran church, one Presbyterian meeting-house, one Quakers ditto, one Anabaptists ditto, one Moravian ditto, and a Jews synagogue. There is also a very handsome charity-school for sixty poor boys and girls, a good work house, barracks for a regiment of soldiers, and one of the finest prisons I have ever seen. . . .

The inhabitants of New York, in their character, very much resemble the Pennsylvanians: more than half of them are Dutch, and almost all traders: they are, therefore, habitually frugal, industrious, and parsimonious. Being, however, of different nations, different languages, and different religions, it is almost impossible to give them any precise or determinate character.[3]

1. Now Columbia University.
2. Mr. Burnaby was an Anglican minister, so only the two Church of England structures counted for him.
3. You can't trust most observers: Burnaby isn't clear here. Half the New Yorkers were Dutch, but not half the Pennsylvanians. Just because it is an original document doesn't mean it is true: sometimes people in the past got things wrong.

9 Flushing Folks Say: "We Protest" to Stuyvesant

The Story of the Flushing Remonstrance

It isn't just Jews who Governor Peter Stuyvesant dislikes: he hates Catholics and Quakers too. Actually he can't stand anyone who doesn't believe as he does. But he feels so strongly about Quakers that in 1656 he has his council pass an ordinance declaring that any person who lets Quakers meet in his or her house will pay a hefty fine. That isn't all. If any ship brings a Quaker into the province that ship will be confiscated.

Now the small town of Flushing on Long Island is part of greater New Amsterdam. The people who founded that town gave it a charter that said its citizens were to have freedom of conscience. In other words, anyone who lives in Flushing will have the right to believe whatever he or she wishes. So when Flushing's citizens hear of Governor Stuyvesant's anti-Quaker ordinance they have a problem. The governor expects them to kick any Quakers out of their town. They aren't going along with that. In 1657 they write an official protest, a legal document called a remonstrance.

Here's a bit of what Flushing's citizens had to say:

"… if any of these said persons come in love unto us, we cannot in conscience lay violent hands upon them, but give them free egresse and regresse unto our Town, and houses, as God shall persuade our consciences. And in this we are true subjects both of Church and State, for we are bounde by the law of God and man to doe good unto all men and evil

"The FLUSHING REMONSTRANCE"

FREEDOM OF RELIGION, GUARANTEED BY OUR BILL OF RIGHTS, WAS BRAVELY DEFENDED 300 YEARS AGO, BY AMERICAN COLONISTS. IN 1656, WHEN NEW YORK WAS A DUTCH COLONY UNDER GOVERNOR PETER STUYVESANT, A LAW WAS PASSED AGAINST THE QUAKERS...

THE TOWNSFOLK OF FLUSHING, LONG ISLAND, WROTE A "REMONSTRANCE" TO THE GOVERNOR-- A PROTEST AGAINST THE LAW...

THE GOVERNOR WILL BE ANGRY AT THOSE WHO SIGN.

WE MUST ALL SIGN. WE MUST SPEAK OUT AGAINST RELIGIOUS INTOLERANCE!

SOME PROMINENT SIGNERS WERE IMPRISONED, AND SOLDIERS WERE SENT TO ENFORCE THE LAW...

THE QUAKERS HELD SECRET MEETINGS IN THE WOODS UNTIL JOHN BOWNE DEFIANTLY OPENED HIS HOME TO THEM. BUT BOWNE'S BOLD PROTEST WAS SEVERELY PUNISHED...

THE GOVERNOR IS SENDING JOHN BOWNE BACK TO HOLLAND TO STAND TRIAL.

HE REFUSED TO PAY A FINE, OR TO ABSTAIN FROM BEFRIENDING QUAKERS. HE SAYS THE LAW IS UNFAIR.

MONTHS LATER, IN HOLLAND...

GENTLEMEN, THIS CHARTER FOR THE TOWN OF FLUSHING GRANTS THE RIGHT FOR LIBERTY OF CONSCIENCE. THE LAW INFRINGES ON THIS RIGHT. THAT IS WHY THE FLUSHING REMONSTRANCE WAS WRITTEN.

HE IS IN THE RIGHT. WE MUST ACQUIT HIM!

TWO YEARS FROM THE TIME OF HIS ARREST, JOHN BOWNE RETURNED TO FLUSHING, A FREE MAN, AND IN 1667...

HAVE YOU HEARD ABOUT THE NEW LAW?

YES, AFTER YEARS OF STRUGGLE, RELIGIOUS FREEDOM IS THE LAW FOR OUR ENTIRE COLONY--THANKS TO BRAVERY AMONG OUR PEOPLE.

LIKE THESE MEN AND WOMEN OF COURAGE, WE IN AMERICA TODAY MUST STAND READY TO PROTECT FREEDOM OF RELIGION FOR ALL--AS PART OF OUR GREAT HERITAGE!

PUBLISHED AS A PUBLIC SERVICE IN COOPERATION WITH THE NATIONAL SOCIAL WELFARE ASSEMBLY, COORDINATING ORGANIZATION FOR NATIONAL HEALTH, WELFARE AND RECREATION AGENCIES OF THE U.S.,

DC Comics published this "news" in September, 1970

to noe man. And this is according to the patent and charter of our Town."

Peter Stuyvesant, being the bully that he is, doesn't pay attention to their remonstrance. And he doesn't change his ordinance. Flushing's citizens don't change either. They decide to test Stuyvesant's edict. They intend that their town be open to all decent folks, no matter what their personal beliefs are.

In 1662, John Bowne openly allows Quakers to worship in his home. What does the governor do? He has Bowne arrested and fined. What happens next? Bowne refuses to back down. He argues in a Dutch court for the religious freedom guaranteed in Flushing's original charter, and the judges agree. Bowne ends up returning home to New Netherland in 1664 both triumphant and a free man.

The original Flushing Remonstrance eventually made its way to the New York State Library in Albany. A fire there in 1911 left its edges blackened. Today it's a treasure of American history and can be found in the Capitol's archieves. My favorite lines in it say, "We desire not to judge lest we be judged, neither to condemn lest we be condemned... we are bound by the law to do good unto all men..."

Remonstrance

Of the Inhabitants of the Town of Flushing To
Governor Stuyvesant

December 27, 1657

Right Honorable,

You have been pleased to send up unto us a certain
prohibition or command that we should not receive or
entertain any of those people called Quakers because they
are supposed to be by some, seducers of the people. For our
part we cannot condemn them in this case, neither can we
stretch out our hands against them, to punish, banish or
persucute them, for out of Christ god is a consuming fire,
and it is a fearful thing to fall into the hands of the living
God.

We desire therefore in this case not to judge least we be
judged, neither to condemn least we be condemned, but
rather let every man stand and fall to his own Master. Wee
are bounde by the Law to doe good unto all men, especially
to those of the household of faith. And though for the
present we seem to be unsensible of the law and the Law
giver, yet when death and the Law assault us, if wee have
our advocate to seeke, who shall plead for us in this case of
conscience betwixt god and our own souls; the power of
this world can neither attack us, neither excuse us, for if
God justifye who can condemn and if God condemn there
is none can justifye.

And for those jealousies and suspicions which some have

of them, that they are destructive unto Magistracy and Ministerye, that can not bee, for the magistarte hath the sword in his hand and the minister hath the sword in his hand, as witnesse those two great examples which all magistrates and ministers are to follow, Moses and Christ, whom god raised up maintained and defended against all the enemies both of flesh and spirit; and therefore that which is of God will stand, and that which is of man will come to nothing. And as the Lord hath taught Moses or the civil power to give an outward liberty in the state by the law written in his heart designed for the good of all, and can truly judge who is good, who is civil, who is true and who is false, and can pass definitive sentence of life or death against that man which rises up against the fundamental law of the States General; soe he hath made his ministers a savor of life unto life, and a savor of death unto death.

The law of love, peace and liberty in the states extending to Jews, Turks, and Egyptians, as they are considered the sonnes of Adam, which is the glory of the outward state of Holland, soe love, peace and liberty, extending to all in Christ Jesus, condemns hatred, war and bondage. And because our Saviour saith it is impossible but that offenses will come, but woe unto him by whom they cometh, our desire is not to offend one of his little ones, in whatsoever form, name or title hee appears in, whether Presbyterian, Independent, Baptist or Quaker, but shall be glad to see anything of God in any of them, desiring to doe unto all men as wee desire all men should doe unto us, which is the true law both of Church and State; for our Saviour saith this is the law and the prophets.

Therefore if any of these said persons come in love unto us, we cannot in conscience lay violent hands upon them, but give them free egresse and regresse unto our Town, and houses, as God shall persuade our consciences. And in this we are true subjects both of Church and State, for we are bounde by the law of God and man to doe good unto all men and evil to noe man. And this is according to the patent and charter of our Towne, given unto us in the name of the States General, which we are not willing to infringe, and violate, but shall houlde to our patent anmd shall remaine, your humble servants, the inhabitants of Vlishing.

Written this 27th day of December, in the year 1657, by mee
EDWARD HART, Clericus
Tobias Feake
Nathaniel Tue
The mark of William Noble
Nicholas Blackford
The mark of Micah Tue
William Thorne, seignor
Antonie Feild
The mark of William Thorne
John Mastine Junior
The mark of Philipp Ud
Richard Stockton
Edward Tarne
John Townesend
Robert Field, senior
Edward Griffine
John Store
Edward Farrington
Robert Field, junior
Nathaniel Hefferd
Nick Colas Parsell
Benjamin Hubbard
Michael Milner
The mark of Henry Townsend
William Pigion
George Wright
The mark of John Foard
George Clere
Henry Semtell

Elias Doughtie
Edward Hart

This is a tough document to read. It is written in 17th century language.
But there are some brilliant statements here. Try and find and highlight
them.

What does "the mark" of John Foard mean? (It means he couldn't sign
his name, so he made an X or some other mark. Why couldn't some of
these citizens sign their names?)

10 Islam: In the New Nation from its Beginnings

Our first president didn't know it, but he almost certainly had Muslims on his plantation. Other slaveholders probably did too. George Washington listed two enslaved West African women as his taxable property in 1784.

A mother and a daughter, they were named "Fatimer" and "Little Fatimer." Fatima was a favorite daughter of the prophet Muhammad. So in the Muslim world, Fatima is an often chosen name for women. A 1721 record of purchase from the Ball plantation near Charleston, South Carolina reads: "Bought Fatima..."

Who was she?

Many of those brought in chains to America were West Africans who came from nations like today's Sierra Leone where Muslims were and are a significant part of the population. Often captured by other Africans, they were sold to slave traders. This was business: it made some Africans rich and it provided enslaved workers in America. Selling slaves was a messy business that brought pain, harm and death to others, but it made a lot of money for the traffickers. That conflict between what is right and what makes money didn't begin or end with slave traders. Do you know examples of that kind of commerce today?

America's founders were well aware of North Africa's Muslim

This monument, along the "Road of Slaves" in the West African country of Benin, commemorates the Africans who were kidnapped and sold as slaves between the 16th and 19th centuries.

nations (often called Barbary Coast nations). In 1777, not long after the Declaration of Independence was signed, General George Washington and the Sultan of Morocco exchanged letters and Morocco became the first country to recognize the United States as an independent nation. Meanwhile American ships sailing in the Mediterranean Sea were getting hijacked by Barbary pirates. Ships and sailors were held for ransom. In March 1785, two years before the Constitution was signed, Thomas Jefferson and John Adams went to London to try and stop that hijacking; they negotiated with Tripoli's ambassador. This is what the ambassador said:

> "It is written in the Koran (Qur'an) that all nations which had not acknowledged the Prophet are sinners… it was the right and duty of the faithful to plunder and enslave...."

The conflict was thought to be settled when the Treaty of Tripoli was signed in Tripoli on November 4, 1796, and also at Algiers on January 3, 1797. Presented to the new U.S. Senate by President John Adams, it was ratified unanimously on June 7, 1797. There's a reason for including it in this book. That treaty, a routine document, included a statement on religion and religious freedom written by American founders. Here it is:

> "As the Government of the United States of America is not, in any sense, founded on the Christian religion; as it has in itself no character of enmity against the laws, religion, or tranquility, of Mussulmen [Muslims]; and as the said States never entered into any war or act of hostility against any Mahometan [Muslim] nation, it is declared by the parties that no pretext arising from religious opinions shall ever produce an interruption of the harmony existing between the two countries."

The American founders were well aware of the centuries of religious war in Europe and the Middle East. If they were going to go to war it would not be over religion. They were clear: this new nation was not founded to support any one religion. Rather, it would be respectful of all.

Unfortunately that reasonable approach didn't work with some zealots who were mostly interested in gold but used religion as a shield for their actions. In 1801 the new nation went to war with the Barbary States (Tripoli, Algiers, Tunis, and Morocco) over acts of piracy.

Ayuba Suleiman Diallo, also known as Job ben Solomon, was a teacher and father of four when he was kidnapped and sold into slavery. After three years in Maryland he was able to get a letter to his father in what is now Senegal. His father 'redeemed' Job - purchased his freedom

11 Catholic Calverts Come to America

Catholics were discriminated against in the British Isles. It had begun when King Henry VIII broke with the Pope and set up his own church, the Anglican Church of England. But many citizens in Ireland, which was part of Great Britain, wanted to stay Catholic and follow the Pope. So they rebelled and made trouble. England's King James I sent George Calvert to Ireland to see if he could get the Irish Catholics to behave. Calvert was wealthy and charming, and everyone liked him. But Calvert surprised the king (and himself too) by becoming a Catholic. He made things difficult for himself when he converted to Catholicism. It was a time when

Catholics were unpopular and persecuted in England. Calvert, being very rich, was able to avoid much of the aggravation, but he knew most of his fellow Catholics couldn't.

So Calvert, who was also known as Lord Baltimore, decided to help British Catholics find a place where they could live without harassment. Like the Puritans, he looked to America. The first American settlement he tried was in Newfoundland. Have you been there? Well, it was too cold for Lord Baltimore.

This postage stamp commemorates the 300th anniversary of the voyage of the *Ark* and *Dove*, ships hired by Cecilus Calvert to bring the first colonists to Maryland

Next he tried Jamestown. Catholics weren't welcome there. Finally the king (now Charles I) gave Calvert a grant of land just north of the Virginia settlements. Calvert named it "Maryland" after King Charles I's wife, Henrietta Maria. George Calvert died before he could get there himself, but his two sons carried on for him. Cecilus Calvert, the new Lord Baltimore, became the proprietor (although he too remained in England). Leonard Calvert became the first actual on-the-site governor.

Like their father, the Calvert sons had ideas that were ahead of the times. They seemed to genuinely believe in toleration. They also knew that Maryland could not survive without Protestants (there just weren't enough Catholics willing to come to America) and they didn't want the Protestant government in England to take back their charter. So Cecilus told his brother Leonard to be careful "to preserve unity and peace amongst all the passengers on Shipp-board, and that they suffer no scandall nor offence to be given to any of the Protestants." In plain words, what Cecilus said to brother Leonard was, "be nice to the Protestants."

Maryland was unique. Nowhere else were Catholics and Protestants attempting to live together in harmony and equality. It wasn't easy. In Europe they'd been killing each other in brutal wars.

Virginia and Massachusetts had established churches and laws about spiritual matters. If you didn't go to church you could get fined, or worse. Everyone paid taxes to support the established church, even if they didn't believe in it.

There was no established church in Maryland and no laws about spiritual matters. At first, both Catholics and Protestants used the same chapel for their worship. The Calverts were remarkable in their even-handed, far-sighted policies. When William Lewis, a

Catholic, tried to convert Protestants he was fined for proselytizing, which means trying to convert others. That was forbidden. But both Catholics and Protestants were encouraged to proselytize among the Indians. (Why? What do you think of that decision?)

The first Maryland settlers arrived in 1633, which was a decade before something astonishing happened in England. **It was the English Civil War, which pitted the king and his Anglican supporters against the Puritans and their leader Oliver Cromwell.** In other words, the English Civil War was mostly about religious power and differences. The king lost, which was hard to believe. England had voted to turn Puritan. That meant Anglicans, Catholics and other non-Puritans were in trouble. Kings were supposed to tell their people what to believe and how to worship. King Charles I could no longer do that. The Calverts had picked a very hard time to start a colony based on religious toleration.

Puritanism was all about peace and love, but the Puritans in January of 1649, led by Oliver Cromwell, beheaded King Charles I in front of a big crowd. Can you imagine? Englishmen killing their king! Some people thought kings had God-given divine rights. Most had been taught to revere their ruler. If you think the world is mixed up and confusing today, try and imagine what it must have been like to people in 1649. Scholarly James Ussher, who was archbishop of the Protestant Church of Ireland, watched the execution and fainted. (Ussher is an interesting fellow. He would be a good subject for research.)

England was now a Commonwealth with Puritans in charge; since most Puritans thought they had the only true path to God, tolerance didn't make sense. That outlook left Cecilus Calvert, a friend of the now-dead king, in danger of losing his colony. His shrewdness helped save things. Cecilus Calvert drafted "An Act

In this woodcut, Charles I loses head and hat. But the king wore a cap, not a hat, and his executioner was masked so citizens wouldn't know who killed their king.

Concerning Religion" which has come to be famous and known as the "Toleration Act."

The Toleration Act said that no person "professing to believe in Jesus Christ shall from henceforth be any way troubled, molested or discountenanced, for or in respect of his or her Religion, nor in the free Exercise thereof. . ." Which is the way things had been in Maryland from its beginnings.

The Maryland General Assembly was now dominated by Puritans; they added a first clause to the Toleration Act calling for the death penalty for anyone who said that Jesus Christ was not the Son of God or for anyone speaking out against the Holy Trinity. (The Trinity is the Christian belief in God as Father, Son and Holy Ghost.) So the Toleration Act did not grant religious liberty or separation of church and state. For Jews, Atheists, or non-Trinitarian Christians, Maryland offered the death penalty. The toleration policy of the Calverts had been more liberal than that of the Toleration Act. Still, it is an important document. It is an official written statement of toleration between Catholics and Protestants. There hadn't been anything like that before.

It was too much for some Puritans, who now felt empowered. Ironically, it was the Calverts' generosity and openness that had helped create the trouble. Because of the Calverts' tolerance many Puritans had settled in the colony during the English Civil War. They became the most powerful faction in the General Assembly. In 1654 the Maryland assembly renounced Lord Baltimore's authority and revoked the Toleration Act, replacing it with one denying protection to Catholics.

But three years later the Calverts were back in power. **They reinstated "An Act Concerning Religion."** However, Catholics did not regain the right to vote in Maryland until after the American Revolution. When Charles Carroll—a Catholic—represented Maryland at the Continental Congress in Philadelphia, he could sign the Declaration of Independence but he could not vote in his own state. (That would soon change.)

In the Name of Religion:

1659. Mary Dyer is hanged for the crime of claiming she was without sin, an opinion said to "overthrow the whole gospel."

1660. William Colburne is fined £100 sterling for showing hospitality to Quakers. (£100 is English money, called pounds. £100 then and now is a lot of money.)

1695. Quaker Thomas Aikenhead, an 18-year-old student, is hanged for denying the truth of the trinity.

12 Pennsylvania Welcomes Everyone to Penn's Woods

Young William Penn was rich, Anglican and a friend of the king. That king was Charles II, who was put on the throne by the same British people who had beheaded his father, Charles I. The experiment that turned Britain into a Puritan nation was finished. Oliver Cromwell's Commonwealth had lasted 19 years. It might have continued if Cromwell's son Richard had been a capable leader, but he wasn't. Besides, under Puritan rule much public fun, like dancing, was outlawed. Some people were ready to have a good time again. The new king Charles II sailed from exile in the Netherlands, landing on English soil on his birthday, May 23, 1660. It would be known as "Restoration Day."

British citizens who longed for kings and queens and their pageantry were happy. So were some who wanted power and got it, and others who wanted revenge against those who had killed Charles I. The English, Scottish and Irish monarchies were all restored. **The Anglican Church was back as the national church in England.** All this was messy and involved some fighting. After it was over, a few people danced around maypoles taunting the Presbyterians and Independents who seemed to have lost out. Charles II, who was known as the "merry monarch," may have been the right person for the time. He didn't bother much about government issues.

Let's get back to William Penn. His father, an admiral, had been a good friend of Charles I. So William was welcome in the royal palace even though Penn had become a member of a radical outcast sect, the Society of Friends (also known as Quakers). Quakers, taking Christ's words literally, believe in peaceful ways and in loving their neighbors—no matter who those neighbors are or what they believe. Quakers think every person can be his own minister, so they have no regular ministers. They believe all people are equal in the sight of God.

In William Penn's day, some people—like ministers, kings, lords, and dukes—were considered superior to the average person. They expected others to bow to them. They were called "betters." The Quakers said all people are equal before God. They wouldn't bow down to anyone. They refused to pay taxes to support the newly restored Church of England. Can you see why they were a problem? The Quakers were a threat to everyone who felt comfortable with the established ways of doing things. New ideas are often dreaded. Quakers were persecuted and killed because of their ideas.

What did being a Quaker do for wealthy William Penn? It got him kicked out of college when he refused to attend Anglican prayers. It led him to jail—for his beliefs—more than once. It gave him a faith that he carried through his life. And it also gave him a reason for founding an American colony.

King Charles II liked William Penn in spite of his religion. Everyone, it seems, was charmed by his sweet ways. But when Penn came before the King and refused to take off his hat—Quakers defer only to God—there were those who gasped and wondered if Penn's head, along with his hat, might be removed. But the "merry monarch" must have been in a good mood because, as the story goes, he laughed and doffed his own hat saying, "Only one head can be covered in the presence of a King."

William Penn and Charles II speak in the king's breakfast room. Note where most of the people are looking. Were they worried about Penn keeping his head?

Now King Charles had borrowed money from Admiral Penn, and a goodly sum it must have been. After the admiral died, his son William asked that the debt be paid with land in America. And so it was—with a vast tract of land spread out midway between the pious Puritans to the North and the convivial Anglican tobacco and rice planters to the South.

Quakers weren't wanted in either of those regions: they were jailed or banished in Massachusetts and Virginia. William Penn saw that Quakers had their own colony, but he made it different from most of the other colonies. Penn really believed in brotherly love. He said that Pennsylvania was not just for Quakers; Pennsylvania was for everyone, and that included people from Africa.

A Record of the Monthly Meeting of the Germantown, Pennsylvania Mennonites

February 18, 1688

(This document deals with a profound problem that will haunt the American nation. here it is called "the traffic of men-body" which means slaves.)

These are the reasons why we are against the traffic of men-body, as followeth: Is there any that would be done or handled at this manner? viz., to be sold or made a slave for all the time of his life? …Now, though they are black, we cannot conceive there is more liberty to have them slaves, as it is to have other white ones. There is a saying that we should do to all men like as we will be done ourselves; making no difference of what generation, descent, or colour they are. And those who steal or rob men, and those who buy or purchase them are they not all alike? Here is liberty of conscience, which is right and reasonable; here ought to be likewise liberty of body, except of evil-doers, which is another case. But to bring men hither, or to rob and sell them against their will, we stand against. In Europe there are many oppressed for conscience-sake; and here there are those oppressed which are of a black colour….Ah! do consider well this thing, you who do it, if you would be done at this manner—and if it is done according to Christianity! You surpass Holland and Germany in this thing. This makes an ill report in all those countries of Europe, where they hear of (it), that the Quakers do here handel men as they handel there the cattle. And for that reason some have no mind or inclination to come hither. And who shall maintain this your cause, or plead for it? Truly, we cannot do so, except you shall inform us better hereof, viz.: that christians have liberty to practice these things. Pray, what thing in the world can be done worse towards us, than if men should rob or steal us away, and sell us for slaves to strange countries; separating husbands from their wives and children. Being now this is not done in the manner we would be done at; therefore, we contradict, and are against this traffic of men-body. And we who profess that it is not lawful to steal, must likewise avoid to purchase such things as are stolen, but rather help to stop this robbing and stealing, if possible. And such men ought to be delivered out of the hands of the robbers, and set free as in Europe. Then is Pennsylvania to have a good report, instead, it hath now a bad one, for this sake, in other countries; Especially whereas the Europeans are desirous to know in what manner the Quakers do rule in their province; and most of them do look upon us with an envious eye. But if this is done well, what shall we say is done evil?

If once these slaves (which they say are so wicked and stubborn men,) should join themselves—fight for their freedom, and handel their masters and mistresses, as they did handel them before; will these masters and mistresses take the sword at hand and war against these poor slaves, like, as we are able to believe, some will not refuse to do?…

Now consider well this thing, if it is good or bad. And in case you find it to be good to handel these blacks in that manner, we desire and require you hereby lovingly, that you may inform us herein, which at this time never was done, viz., that Christians have such a liberty to do so. To the end we shall be satisfied on this point, and satisfy likewise our good friends and acquaintances in our native country, to whom it is a terror, or fearful thing, that men should be handelled so in Pennsylvania.

This from our meeting at Germantown, held ye 18th of the
2d month, 1688, to be delivered to the monthly meeting at
Richard Worrell's.
Garret Henderich
Derick of de Graeff
Francis Daniel Pastorius
Abram of de Graeff

When you see three dots ("...") in an original document it means
that words have been cut out. Maybe it was too long; maybe there
are other reasons. You can find this document on the web if you
want to read the whole version.

In this document you can follow the thoughts of four men
struggling with a profound problem. What is it? Why was it
difficult? What is the point they are making? Pull out two or three
key sentences to illustrate your answers.

13 Two Big Minds Write About Toleration (1651-92)

Thomas Hobbes and **John Locke** were English contemporaries of the Puritans. They were philosophers (deep thinkers) who helped create the world we live in today. Hobbes wrote a book in 1651 called *Leviathan*; it would become the foundation of much of Western political thinking. He said that nations and their citizens are joined in a "social contract" which gives each of them rights and responsibilities. While citizens owe absolute support to the king and his church (said Hobbes), the king's power rests on the consent of the people. This idea of "consent of the people," in a world emerging from feudalism, was huge. Most kings hadn't considered the idea that their power depended on the will of the people. Most talked about divine right and believed it was God, not the people, who had made them rulers.

Hobbes had another thought that was amazing in its time: he realized that kings can force action but they can't force beliefs. So they shouldn't try, he said. Individuals should be allowed to hold their own religious beliefs as long as they outwardly support the state church.

Thirty-eight years after *Leviathan*, Locke published *A Letter Concerning Toleration*. Actually, it was a letter Locke wrote to his close friend Philipp van Limborch, who published it without Locke's knowledge. It became enormously influential. A hundred years later, Thomas Jefferson and all of America's founders read that letter. In it, Locke proposed religious toleration as a way to end much of the conflict in the world he knew.

After centuries of religious wars and political turmoil, Locke argued that by tolerating different religions a state can actually prevent protests and war. Roger Williams, who was Locke's contemporary and friend, agreed. Remember, he said, "forced worship stinks in God's nostrils." Williams understood that you may be able to force people to go to church, but you can't force them to believe. That seems obvious to most of us, but it was a difficult issue at a time when most people thought there was only one true belief and one true church.

Toleration was essential for Locke, who seemed to have uncertainties about the idea of one true religion. But he didn't include atheists and Catholics in his toleration concept. He didn't think they could be good citizens within a state. In later writings he changed his mind a bit on that. His transformative ideas had to incubate and evolve.

A century later, James Madison and some of his colleagues questioned the word "toleration" because it suggests that there is only one truth, that some humans have found it, and that all other ideas need to be "tolerated" or "endured." **At the time Hobbes and Locke were writing, toleration was a new concept and it was not well received by most Puritans.** "Why should we tolerate ideas that aren't true?" they asked, never considering that they might not know what is true.

Question: What is truth? Today most of us believe that no human knows absolute truth, but that its pursuit is a worthwhile journey for societies and people that embark on it with open minds. John Locke, from his *Letter Concerning Toleration*:

> "The political society is instituted for no other end, but only to secure every man's possession of the things of this life. The care of each man's soul and

of the things of heaven, which neither does belong to the commonwealth nor can be subjected to it, is left entirely to every man's self."

14 Wake Up and Listen to the Preacher

Imagine you are a Puritan living in 18th century Massachusetts; you and your family work hard all week, but on Sunday you don't work. It is a day of rest and prayer. You spend most of it in church. The minister takes his sermon from a passage in the Bible. He is a scholarly man and what he says demands close attention. Sometimes he talks for several hours.

Is it boring? Well, some people fall asleep. Children sometimes make faces at each other, or wiggle about, or wish they could be somewhere playing. Some of the adults feel the same way.

But not when they listen to Jonathan Edwards. He is the preacher in Northampton, Massachusetts and he has charisma and energy. Edwards preaches sermons that are filled with fire and brimstone. Which means he talks about Hell and what might happen to those who don't have faith. He also speaks out about "the time of extraordinary dullness in religion" (he's talking about his own time) and the need for preachers to find ways to capture their listeners. Edwards writes an influential book about his ideas; it lays groundwork for a change in preaching styles. That change is known as America's First Great Awakening and it begins after 1739.

That's when George Whitefield arrives in Pennsylvania and begins to preach. Whitefield is 24, a graduate of Oxford University and a friend of John Wesley. These two, along with Wesley's brother Charles, are credited with founding the evangelical movement

WHITEFIELD Preaching

Crowds gathered to hear Whitefield, as seen in this engraving from around 1740

known as Methodism. Evangelicals have strong beliefs relating to personal salvation; those ideas are based on the Christian Gospels.

Whitefield preaches wherever there are people, which often means outdoors. Sometimes he stands on the steps of public buildings rather than in a church. That causes controversy. But people flock to hear him. Whitefield is slim with a strong mellow voice, perfect diction, and an emotion-filled message. Ben Franklin, who hears him speak to a large crowd, says, "It seemed as if all the world were growing religious." The young minister makes a triumphant journey from one colony to another. Soon other strong voices are doing the same kind of preaching.

In the South, most slave owners have little interest in sharing their religion with those they've enslaved. But the new preachers (especially the Baptists and Methodists) are interested in saving souls and eager to convert blacks to Christianity. Along with

African Americans they bring other outsiders into their churches.

This lithograph shows Juliann Jane Tillman, a preacher of the A.M.E. church.

The First Great Awakening is a big success. Suddenly there are a lot of new churches; those churches need ministers, which means there is a need for higher education. Soon there are new colleges. Mostly the evangelical ministers preach a personal religion; they expect people to take charge of their own lives. And that creates independent thinkers, which helps a lot when some leaders decide to break away from England and create a new nation.

Eighteenth century colonists in Massachusetts think they have little in common with those in Virginia or South Carolina. But when the Great Awakening comes along it helps establish a national identity. The Great Awakening is a shared experience that brings the colonies together. That will help make a break from Great Britain possible. It also empowers thinkers who, encouraged to choose their own path to God, believe they can choose their own form of government.

In Boston you can see this statue of Phillis Wheatley on the mall on Commonwealth Avenue. More about her in the next chapter.

15 When Worshipping God was a Black and White Issue

Phillis Wheatley was born in 1743 in West Africa; that same year, Lemuel Haynes was born in Connecticut. Each would bring intellectual gifts, anti-slavery fervor, and deep religious convictions to the soon-to-be-created United States.

Wheatley is eight years old when she arrives in America on a slave ship. Bought by a Boston family, she is given an education unlikely for a slave, or a female, or most colonists (she reads Greek, Latin, and some Hebrew). Later her published poems bring her fame in England (where she meets the Lord Mayor of London) and in the American colonies, where, in 1776, George Washington invites her to visit his headquarters in Cambridge, Mass.

Lemuel Haynes is born to a white mother and black father, who sell him at five months into indentured servitude. Under the agreement he will be educated, taken to church, and freed at 21. So he is a free man in 1775 when he joins a militia company and fights with the Revolutionary forces.

After the war he becomes the first black person to serve as pastor of a white congregation and the first African American ordained as a Christian minister. His writings on theology bring him international fame. For thirty years he is the preacher at Rutland, Vermont's Congregational West Parish (through the administrations of Washington, Adams, Jefferson, and Madison); his dynamic preaching draws crowds.

This serving tray shows an enthusiastic Lemuel Haynes giving a sermon in 1814. Historians believe this was the first time a black minister had preached to a mostly white congregation.

Haynes writes extensively on slavery and the slave trade. "Liberty is equally precious to a black man, as it is to a white one, and bondage is equally as intolerable to the one as to the other," he says.

While in Rutland, he preaches more than 5,000 sermons, and officiates at over 400 funerals and more than 100 marriages. Middlebury College (nearby in Vermont) awards Haynes an honorary Master of Arts degree in 1804; it is the first advanced degree bestowed on an African American in the United States.

For the last 11 years of Haynes' life his home was in South Granville, New York; today it is a National Historic Landmark.

Meanwhile in the South

Where was the first established black church in the United States? First African Baptist Church in Savannah, Georgia claims that title. Officially organized in 1788, it grew out of a congregation of worshippers founded in 1733 by a slave preacher.

During the post-Civil War era of segregation (until the Civil Rights movement brought changes) Savannah's black high school graduates were not allowed to march with their graduating class. Their separate ceremonies were held at First African Baptist Church.

16 Virginia's Baptists Demand Equality

Virginia's Baptists flooded the state assembly with petitions entreating lawmakers to guarantee religious equality. Virginia's House of Burgesses had been established in 1619, just a dozen years after the original settlement at Jamestown. By law, all its members had to be members of the Anglican Church. But the American Revolution put the English church in a strange position.

In 1776, the Virginia General Assembly received a petition signed by 10,000 Baptists, Presbyterians, Quakers, Mennonites and other religious dissenters. They asked for disestablishment of the tax-supported Church of England and that all religious denominations enjoy equal freedom and privileges. Then they added a huge idea. They said making anyone pay taxes to support a church they didn't believe in—well, that was an attack on their freedom to believe as their minds and hearts told them.

Those religious dissenters, who some saw as outcasts, or cultists, or nonconformists, would ally themselves with some deep thinkers. Our country's founders were building a nation on an important idea, one that other thinkers had talked and written about: freedom of conscience or belief. Our Constitution made it the law of the land.

Here it is: all people are born with certain "natural" rights, like the right to "life, liberty, and the pursuit of happiness." These rights don't belong to governments; they belong to individuals. Which means your freedom to believe in a religion, or none, is a right nature has given you. (That's why we call it a "natural" right). Kings and governments don't own those rights, so they can't grant them or take them away, although many rulers have attempted to do just that.

The First Amendment to the Constitution says: "Congress shall make no law respecting an establishment of religion, or prohibiting the free exercise thereof; or abridging the freedom of speech…" It does not "give" Americans religious freedom or freedom of speech; the Founders believed that citizens already have those rights and that it is not government's role to meddle with them. James Madison wrote the First Amendment (part of the Bill of Rights) to protect your natural rights.

The Ninth Amendment makes that clear. It says any rights not listed in the Constitution are "retained by the people" (not by the government).

In a book titled *The Rights of the People*, David K. Shipler says, "In many other constitutions, governments give rights; in the United States Constitution, the people do the giving, by retaining their rights and granting government limited powers."

Does God have any role in this? Decide that for yourself: you have a natural right to do so.

Letter From Virginia's Baptists

It was 1776 and the English Church was being thrown out of the colonies (along with British rule). In this letter the Baptists say it is time to do away with an established church and have religious liberty.

To the Honourable the President and House of Delegates
The Petition of the Dissenters from the
Ecclesiastical establishment in the
Commonwealth of Virginia
Humbly sheweth

That your Petitioners being in common with the other Inhabitants of this Commonwealth delivered from British Oppression rejoice in the Prospect of that having their Freedom secured and maintained to them and their posterity inviolate. The hopes of your petitioners have been raised and confirmed by the Declaration of your Honourable House with regard to equal Liberty. Equal Liberty! that invaluable blessing: which though it be the birth right of every good Member of the State has been what your Petitioners have been Deprived of, in that, by Taxation their property hath been wrested from them and given to those from whom they have received no equivalent.

Your Petitioners therefore having long groaned under the Burden of an Ecclesiastical Establishment beg leave to move your Honourable House that this as well as every other Yoke may be broken and that the Oppressed may go free: that so every religious Denomination being on a Level, Animosities may cease, and that Christian Forbearance, Love and Charity, may be practiced towards each other, while the Legislature interferes only to support them in their just Rights and equal privileges.

17 Thomas Jefferson's Statute For Religious Freedom

Thomas Jefferson is in France as America's first ambassador when, on January 16, 1786, his good friend James Madison gets the Virginia General Assembly to adopt *A Statute for Religious Freedom*. Jefferson had written the bill nine years earlier and then introduced it into the legislature.

Getting it passed was, said Jefferson, "the severest contest in which I have ever been engaged." Among the things the statute says is that any citizen, of any religion, can be a member of the Virginia General Assembly. Jefferson was asking the legislators, who were all Anglican, to open their doors to others of other religions. They voted against his bill, again and again.

Religious freedom for a whole state was an untried idea; no nation had ever put that into its laws. It involved a bothersome issue: shouldn't a state provide religious guidance to its citizens, much as parents to their children? That was what kings did; that was the way it was in England and France and had been in Virginia and the other colonies. But, as a popular song said after the American Revolution, the world had turned upside down. When the newly formed United States signed the Treaty of Paris with Great Britain, officially ending the Revolutionary War, most Anglican priests headed home to England. Something had to be done in the newly united states. Ministers were needed. From where would they come? Baptist and Methodist ministers on horseback were riding through Virginia preaching; because they weren't Anglican that was against the law. They often ended up in jail.

Jefferson's statute, separating church and state, would end that practice: it would allow people to decide religious matters for themselves. If they didn't want to go to church they didn't have to go.

That was too much for many Virginians. George Washington was concerned. If Virginians weren't made to go to church would they become immoral? Patrick Henry, arguing against the idea of religious freedom, introduced a bill into the General Assembly that would establish a general tax to fund all Christian churches. Henry was a popular leader; his bill passed its first two readings. Passage on its third and final reading seemed a certainty.

From France Jefferson wrote to Madison, "What we have to do, I think, is devotedly pray for his death." He was talking about Patrick Henry and he may have had his tongue in his cheek. Madison was more pragmatic. He got Henry kicked upstairs into the governor's chair where he had no veto. Then Madison wrote *A Remonstrance Against Religious Assessments*, a reasoned argument against all forms of religious tyranny (an amazing document and worth researching).

Finally, with the help of Baptists, Methodists and those others who had felt the sting of persecution, Madison, a master politician, guided the bill through the legislature.

Jefferson was in France when he learned of its passage. He was so delighted he had copies of the statute made and he sent them to Europeans he wished to impress with the good judgment of the new nation. Writing to Madison he said, **"It is honorable for us, to have produced the first legislature with the courage to declare that the reason of man may be trusted with the formation of his own opinions."** He had reason to be pleased.

Rembrandt Peale completed this portrait of Jefferson in 1800

That bill is the first in Western history to outlaw religious discrimination. After it passes, Virginia can no longer order its citizens to pay taxes to support a state church. Nor can the state make it a crime not to go to church (as it had previously). Nor mandate that only members of an approved church can be elected or appointed to public office. To repeat: in the past, only

Anglicans had been able to hold office and vote. Amazingly, it is an all-Anglican General Assembly that has voted to allow others to be full citizens and believe as they wish (except for women, children and slaves).

In his statute Jefferson pours forth all his feelings about the corruption and meanness associated with alliances of church and state. It is as much eloquent manifesto as landmark legislation. "To compel a man to furnish contributions of money for the propagation of opinions which he disbelieves, is sinful and tyrannical," he writes. And, "to suffer the civil magistrate to intrude his powers into the field of opinion... is a dangerous fallacy, which at once destroys all religious liberty."

Then Jefferson gets to the substance of the act, **"That no man shall be compelled to frequent or support any religious worship, place, or ministry whatsoever, nor shall be enforced, restrained, molested, or burthened in his body or goods, nor shall otherwise suffer on account of his religious opinions or beliefs..."**

Back in 1776 Jefferson had addressed the Virginia General Assembly and asked this question, "Has the state a right to adopt an opinion on matters of religion?" Then he answered with a strong negative. Men are answerable for their religion solely to God. History shows that religious establishments are always oppressive, he told the legislators. In Virginia, he reminded them, laws on the books made it a criminal offense to deny the validity of the Trinity, heresy was punishable by death, and freethinkers might have their children taken from them. That these laws were rarely enforced was not the point, he said. Besides, they all knew of cases of persecution, especially of Baptist preachers.

Later, writing in *Notes on Virginia*, he continued: **"The**

If you visit Jefferson's grave at Monticello, the monument you see isn't the first marker placed on the former president's grave. Early visitors, eager for souvenirs, chipped off pieces of stone, damaging the obelisk. Jefferson's decendants donated the original monument to the University of Missouri, where it resides at the Francis Quadrangle, as pictured above.

legitimate powers of government extend to such acts only as are injurious to others. But it does me no injury for my neighbor to say there are twenty gods or no god. It neither picks my pocket nor breaks my leg."

Bernard Bailyn, one of Harvard's great American historians, has called the Virginia Statute for Religious Freedom "the most important document in American history, bar none." Unlike Jefferson's great declaration, the statute is an original work of political theory. Jefferson never had any doubt about its importance. When he left handwritten instructions for his tombstone they said, "On the face of the obelisk, the following inscription, and not a word more, 'Here was buried Thomas Jefferson, author of the Declaration of American Independence, of the statute of Virginia for religious freedom, and father of the University of Virginia,' by these as testimonials that I have lived, I wish to be remembered."

He had been governor of Virginia, America's first secretary of state, ambassador to France, and president of the nation, but he wanted to be remembered as author of two great political works as well as founder of a great university.

As for George Washington, after the statute becomes law he finds that Virginians are no more or less moral than they had been before. Washington becomes a big champion of religious freedom. Does Jefferson's hostility to a marriage of church and state include hostility to religion? Merrill Peterson, a biographer, wrote this, "His hatred of establishments and priesthoods did not involve him in a hatred of religion. He wished for himself, for his countrymen, not freedom from religion but freedom to pursue religion wherever intelligence and conscience led.

Virginia Statute for Religious Freedom

Adopted 1785

Well aware that the opinions and belief of men depend not on their own will, but follow involuntarily the evidence proposed to their minds; that Almighty God hath created the mind free, and manifested his supreme will that free it shall remain by making it altogether insusceptible of restraint; that all attempts to influence it by temporal punishments, or burthens, or by civil incapacitations, tend only to beget habits of hypocrisy and meanness, and are a departure from the plan of the holy author of our religion, who being lord both of body and mind, yet chose not to propagate it by coercions on either, as was in his Almighty power to do, but to extend it by its influence on reason alone; that the impious presumption of legislators and rulers, civil as well as ecclesiastical, who, being themselves but fallible and uninspired men, have assumed dominion over the faith of others, setting up their own opinions and modes of thinking as the only true and infallible,and as such endeavoring to impose them on others, hath established and maintained false religions over the greatest part of the world and through all time: That to compel a man to furnish contributions of money for the propagation of opinions which he disbelieves and abhors, is sinful and tyrannical; that even the forcing him to support this or that teacher of his own religious persuasion, is depriving him of the comfortable liberty of giving his contributions to the particular pastor whose morals he would make his pattern, and whose powers he feels most persuasive to righteousness; and is withdrawing from the ministry those temporary rewards, which proceeding from an approbation of their personal conduct, are an additional incitement to earnest and unremitting labours for the instruction of mankind; that our civil rights have no dependance on our religious opinions, any more than our opinions in physics or geometry; that therefore the proscribing any citizen as unworthy the public confidence by laying upon him an incapacity of being called to offices of trust and emolument, unless he profess or renounce this or that religious opinion, is depriving him injuriously of those privileges and advantages to which, in common with his fellow citizens, he has a natural right; that it tends also to corrupt the principles of that very religion it is meant to encourage, by bribing, with a monopoly of worldly honours and emoluments, those who will externally profess and conform to it; that though indeed these are criminal who do not withstand such temptation, yet neither are those innocent who lay the bait in their way; that the opinions of men are not the object of civil government, nor under its jurisdiction; that to suffer the civil magistrate to intrude his powers into the field of opinion and to restrain the profession or propagation of principles on supposition of their ill tendency is a dangerous falacy, which at once destroys all religious liberty, because he being of course judge of that tendency will make his opinions the rule of judgment, and approve or condemn the sentiments of others only as they shall square with or differ from his own; that it is time enough for the rightful purposes of civil government for its officers to interfere when principles break out into overt acts against peace and good order; and finally, that truth is great and will prevail if left to herself; that she is the proper and sufficient antagonist to error, and has nothing to fear from the conflict unless by human interposition disarmed of her natural weapons, free argument and debate; errors ceasing to be dangerous when it is permitted freely to contradict them.

We the General Assembly of Virginia do enact that no man

shall be compelled to frequent or support any religious worship, place, or ministry whatsoever, nor shall be enforced, restrained, molested, or burthened in his body or goods, nor shall otherwise suffer, on account of his religious opinions or belief; but that all men shall be free to profess, and by argument to maintain, their opinions in matters of religion, and that the same shall in no wise diminish, enlarge, or affect their civil capacities.

And though we well know that this Assembly, elected by the people for the ordinary purposes of legislation only, have no power to restrain the acts of succeeding Assemblies, constituted with powers equal to our own, and that therefore to declare this act irrevocable would be of no effect in law; yet we are free to declare, and do declare, that the rights hereby asserted are of the natural rights of mankind, and that if any act shall be hereafter passed to repeal the present or to narrow its operation, such act will be an infringement of natural right.

George Washington's Letter To The Hebrew Congregation of Newport, Rhode Island

1790

George Washington arrived in Newport, Rhode Island on the morning of August 17th, 1790. Secretary of State Thomas Jefferson and some leading government officials came with him. The new president had waited to visit Rhode Island until that state finally ratified the Constitution. Now the Bill of Rights, written by James Madison and guaranteeing religious freedom, needed to be ratified. Rhode Island, thanks to Roger Williams, had a long history in support of that freedom. Washington had originally worried about broad religious freedom; but he had seen its effect in Virginia and was now an ardent enthusiast.

In Newport an admiring crowd turned out to cheer the new president; civic leaders read letters of welcome. One of those leaders, Moses Seixas, was an official of Yeshuat Israel, the first Jewish congregation in Newport. Here is part of his letter to the new president:

Deprived as we heretofore have been of the invaluable rights of free Citizens, we now (with a deep sense of gratitude to the Almighty disposer of all events) behold a Government, erected by the Majesty of the People—a Government, which to bigotry gives no sanction, to persecution no assistance—but generously affording to All liberty of conscience, and immunities of Citizenship: deeming every one, of whatever Nation, tongue, or language, equal parts of the great governmental Machine…

George Washington had been a member of the Church of England; now with England officially gone from the new nation, he was an Episcopalian. He had worried that a nation that didn't force its citizens to go to church might expect a lot of immoral behavior. But the success of the *Virginia Statute for Religious Freedom* made him realize that citizens can be trusted to think for themselves, especially about matters of heart and soul.
He now believed that certain human rights are "inalienable," which means those rights belong to persons and should be beyond the power of nations or kings or presidents to bestow or take away. This was more than toleration. It was about real respect for the ideas of others.

So, the new nation had no official church. This was an exciting but untried concept. Here are the first president's words about it in a famous letter he wrote to the members of the Hebrew Congregation in Newport, Rhode Island on August 18, 1790:

Gentlemen:
While I received with much satisfaction your address replete with expressions of esteem, I rejoice in the opportunity of assuring you that I shall always retain grateful remembrance of the cordial welcome I experienced on my visit to Newport from all classes of citizens.

The reflection on the days of difficulty and danger which are past is rendered the more sweet from a consciousness that they are succeeded by days of uncommon prosperity and security.

If we have wisdom to make the best use of the advantages with which we are now favored, we cannot fail, under the just administration of a good government, to become a great and happy people.

The citizens of the United States of America have a right to applaud themselves for having given to mankind examples of an enlarged and liberal policy—a policy worthy of imitation. All possess alike liberty of conscience and immunities of citizenship.

It is now no more that toleration is spoken of as if it were the indulgence of one class of people that another enjoyed the exercise of their inherent natural rights, for, happily, the Government of the United States, which gives to bigotry no sanction, to persecution no assistance, requires only that they who live under its protection should demean themselves as good citizens in giving it on all occasions their effectual support.

It would be inconsistent with the frankness of my character not to avow that I am pleased with your favorable opinion of my administration and fervent wishes for my felicity.

May the children of the stock of Abraham who dwell in this land continue to merit and enjoy the good will of the other inhabitants—while every one shall sit in safety under his own vine and fig tree and there shall be none to make him afraid.

May the father of all mercies scatter light, and not darkness, upon our paths, and make us all in our several vocations useful here, and in His own due time and way everlastingly happy.

G. Washington

18 A Constitution and its First Amendment

If anyone can be said to be the father of the U.S. Constitution it is James Madison. With his quiet, efficient way, he is a mastermind at the Constitutional Convention.

One of the big issues at the convention is deciding what power should go to the new federal government and what should remain with the states. The Articles of Confederation gave too much power to the states. But finding a balance isn't easy.

When it comes to guaranteeing basic human rights, like freedom of religion, Madison believes that is up to each state. Virginia has a good bill of rights, written by George Mason, an older statesman everyone admires. Madison thinks other states can do the same thing.

The only words on religion in the newly crafted Constitution are in Article VI. It says that "no religious Test shall ever be required as a Qualification to any Office or public Trust under the United States."

Madison doesn't see any need for the nation's constitution to go further. But many delegates disagree. They won't sign the constitution unless their freedoms are certain. They want a Bill of Rights and they want Madison to write it. He agrees.

Madison's Bill of Rights is in the form of the first ten amendments to the new U.S. Constitution. Today we think of those amendments as central to our democracy and its guarantees of freedom. Madison keeps the amendments simple and to the point.

Here are the First Amendment's words (contrast Madison's style with that of the eloquent but sometimes wordy Thomas Jefferson):

> "Congress shall make no law respecting an establishment of religion, or prohibiting the free exercise thereof; or abridging the freedom of speech, or of the press; or the right of the people peaceably to assemble, and to petition the Government for a redress of grievances."

The first two clauses in that sentence deal with religious freedom. The first is known as the "establishment clause." The second is the "free exercise clause."

They are intended to speak for themselves, but lawmakers in generations to come will often disagree on what was intended. What is clear is that Congress cannot set up, or establish, a national religion. Madison believed there should be strict separation of church and state. In 1791, when this amendment was adopted, most of his peers agreed.

The free exercise clause says when it comes to religion, we citizens are free to practice any belief we choose.

The full First Amendment goes further, protecting speech, journalism, and the ability of the people to gather together and protest against the government. Those rights have defined the United States and its democracy. They are central to our way of life and to our freedoms.

But how do you interpret them? Can a citizen believe one interpretation and the government another? That's where the Supreme Court comes in. Take the issue of religious freedom. We still don't always agree on what that should mean. If you study the Court's cases on religious freedom you'll see freedom ideas evolve. At the same time, the Court often goes back to the Founders' ideas for guidance. In an 1878 case known as *Reynolds v. United States*, the Court quoted an 1802 letter that Thomas Jefferson wrote to a Baptist Church in Danbury, Connecticut, where he said:

> "Believing with you that religion is a matter which lies solely between Man & his God… I contemplate with sovereign reverence that act of the whole American people which declared that their legislature should 'make no law respecting an establishment of religion, or prohibiting the free exercise thereof,' thus building a wall of separation between Church & State."

That image of a wall of separation came from Roger Williams; the Supreme Court has used it in a number of its decisions. (Some people think that wall should be breached; others want to strengthen it.)

In *Gitlow v. New York*, a 1925 case, the Supreme Court made it clear that the First Amendment isn't just law on the Federal level. It also applies within states.

In *Everson v. Board of Education*, a 1947 case, the Court cited Thomas Jefferson's "wall of separation between church and State." But in Everson, the Court permitted New Jersey school boards to pay for transportation to parochial schools. James Madison would probably not have agreed with that decision, but it was made because bus rides were said to neither advance nor inhibit religion.

Key Words from the Danbury Baptists' Letter To Thomas Jefferson

October 7, 1801

Our Sentiments are uniformly on the side of Religious Liberty—That Religion is at all times and places a Matter between God and Individuals—That no man aught to suffer in Name, person or effects on account of his religious Opinions—That the legetimate Power of civil Goverment extends no further than to punish the man who works ill to his neighbour: But Sir, our constitution of goverment is not specific. Our antient charter, together with the Laws made coincident therewith, were adopted as the Basis of our goverment, At the time of our revolution; and such had been our Laws & usages, & such still are; that religion is consider'd as the first object of Legislation; & therefore what religious privileges we enjoy (as a minor part of the State) we enjoy as favors granted, and not as inalienable rights: and these favors we receive at the expence of such degrading acknowledgements as are inconsistant with the rights of freemen.

Nehemiah Dodge
Ephraim Robbins
Steven S. Nelson
(The Committee)

Jefferson's Letter to the Danbury Baptists

January 1, 1802

(Note the phrase "wall of separation;" it will become famous. This letter was written when Jefferson was president).

To messers. Nehemiah Dodge, Ephraim Robbins, & Stephen S. Nelson, a committee of the Danbury Baptist association in the state of Connecticut.

Gentlemen

The affectionate sentiments of esteem and approbation which you are so good as to express towards me, on behalf of the Danbury Baptist association, give me the highest satisfaction. my duties dictate a faithful and zealous pursuit of the interests of my constituents, & in proportion as they are persuaded of my fidelity to those duties, the discharge of them becomes more and more pleasing.

Believing with you that religion is a matter which lies solely between Man & his God, that he owes account to none other for his faith or his worship, that the legitimate powers of government reach actions only, & not opinions, I contemplate with sovereign reverence that act of the whole American people which declared that their legislature should "make no law respecting an establishment of religion, or prohibiting the free exercise thereof," thus building a wall of separation between Church & State. Adhering to this expression of the supreme will of the nation in behalf of the rights of conscience, I shall see with sincere satisfaction the progress of those sentiments which tend to restore to man all his natural rights, convinced he has no natural right in opposition to his social duties.

I reciprocate your kind prayers for the protection & blessing of the common father and creator of man, and tender you for yourselves & your religious association, assurances of my high respect & esteem.

Th Jefferson

19 Wake Up, Again

The Second Great Awakening erupts early in the 19th century. Revivals soon sweep the newly freed nation. Many take place on the frontier, with people coming from far distances to attend. They camp out, sometimes for weeks. For those doing lonely pioneering it's a chance to socialize and share experiences. Some revivals are so large that there are preaching stands with many ministers speaking at the same time, each preaching to those within range of his voice.

The preachers, the good ones, try to include everyone's thoughts and needs in their sermons. Some work their listeners into a frenzy: people shout out and weep. The emphasis is on personal salvation. All this is especially empowering for women who don't often get a chance to participate in public events, or think for themselves. Lots of women convert. The same is true of African Americans who are usually welcome at the revivals.

In 1801, George Baxter, president of Washington College in Virginia, writes this after attending a revival in Kentucky:

> "A religious awe seemed to pervade the country… I think the revival in Kentucky the most extraordinary that has ever visited the Church of Christ… the revival has confounded infidelity, awed vice into silence, and brought numbers beyond calculation under serious impressions… I found Kentucky…the most moral place I have ever been…"

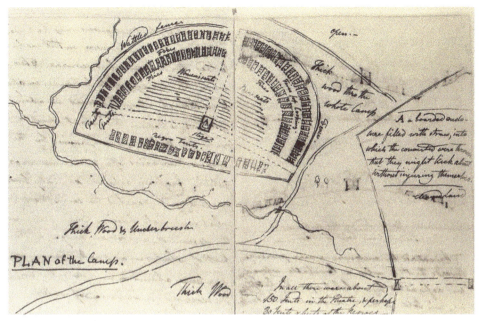

This sketch, by Benjamin Latrobe, shows the plan of an 1809 Methodist camp meeting in Virginia. If you look closely you can see that the men's seats were separated from the women's and the "negro tents" from the whites'. To accommodate the sometimes-uncontrollable emotions generated at camp meetings, Latrobe noted that, at the right of the main camp, the organizers had built a "boarded enclosure filled with straw, into which the converted were thrown that they might kick about without injuring themselves."

Thomas Jefferson sees the evangelicals in a different light. This is what he says in 1822: "The atmosphere of our country is unquestionably charged with a threatening cloud of fanaticism, lighter in some parts, denser in others..."

Jefferson, who attends church often, was raised in the Church of England. After the Revolution he attends Episcopalian services or non-denominational services in the House of Representatives. Jefferson contributes regularly to the churches he attends. He is fascinated by religious concepts and owns and reads a copy of the Muslim Qur'an.

But he never stops thinking for himself. Here is something he writes in his book, *Notes on the State of Virginia*:

"Millions of innocent men, women and children, since the introduction of Christianity, have been burnt, tortured, fined and imprisoned; yet we have not advanced one inch towards uniformity. What has been the effect of coercion? To make one half the world fools, and the other half hypocrites. To support roguery and error all over the earth."

And here is something he says in a letter to a friend (Roger Weightman):

"All eyes are opened, or opening, to the rights of man. The general spread of the light of science has already laid open to every view the palpable truth, that the mass of mankind has not been born with saddles on their backs, nor a favored few booted and spurred, ready to ride them legitimately, by the grace of God."

(Saddles on their backs? He is talking about poor people and especially slaves. He disapproves of those saddles but has no solution to the problems of poverty or slavery)

20 Manumission: A Word that Takes a Sad Story and Gives it a Happy Ending

It is 1749 and Robert Carter III has just turned 21, which means he is able to access his inhereitance: money, land, and enslaved workers left to him by his father and grandfather. As soon as he has control of his fortune, he sails to England with his friend Lawrence Washington (George's half brother).

When he arrives in London, Carter heads for the swankiest tailor in town. That tailor makes him a gold suit with a lace collar and a silver cape; then he has his portrait painted. He looks posh and regal in that painting; it is the only picture we have of him.

Young Robert Carter is rich. Not just ordinarily rich, but very rich: he has more enslaved workers on his plantations than any of his contemporaries.

Carter's grandfather was the famous (maybe infamous) "King" Carter, the wealthiest man in Virginia. A long time member of the House of Burgesses, and a colonial governor, he was known for his brilliance as an entrepreneur and also for his autocratic ways. He expected to get his way, and he usually did.

The "King" and his son, Robert II, die within months of each other (Robert II of an opium overdose). Robert III is four years old; in the years ahead he will have no father or grandfather to guide him. So it may not be a surprise that he becomes spoiled, arrogant and undisciplined. When it comes to book learning he doesn't do much because he doesn't want to.

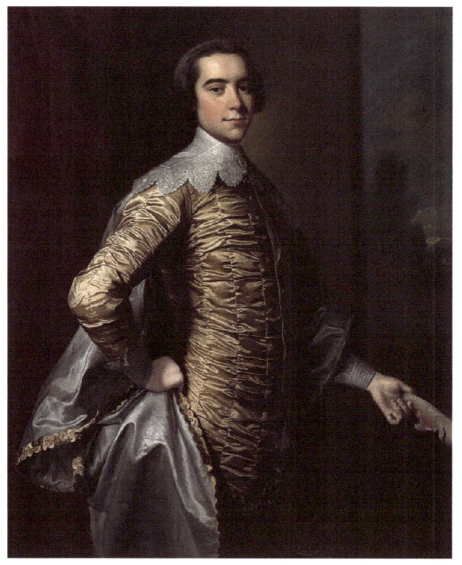

Robert Carter III, painted by Thomas Hudson in 1753

He goes to London, he says, to study law and make business contacts, but mostly he joins other rowdy Americans in having what they see as a good time. A British author, Edward Kimber writes a novel about a slaveholding American who visits London. That character, whom he names "Carter," is described as "a lad of bad principles, unlettered, and of coarse manners." In the book a slave murders him. The novel's readers may have cheered.

When Robert Carter III returns to Virginia he carries on as he had in London: mainly doing whatever he wants to do. He moves from the Carter plantation on Virginia's Northern Neck to nearby Williamsburg where he expects to get elected to the House of Burgesses (like his father and grandfather), but he gets fewer votes than any other candidate.

And then he changes. He begins to read deeply, think passionately, and act courageously. His personal library becomes one of the largest on the continent; he devours books on history, philosophy, law and religion. Carter becomes a deep thinker who discusses books and ideas with Virginia intellectuals at the College of William and Mary (including George Wythe and young Tom Jefferson). What accounts for his change? No one is quite sure but two influences have come into his life.

One is a wife. Robert Carter falls in love with Frances Ann Tasker, the daughter of a Maryland governor. They stay in love all their lives, have 17 children (five die before adulthood), and share books, ideas, and faith. Carter will say that his wife is better read than the minister at Williamsburg's Anglican Church (who is supposed to be an intellectual).

The other influence is spiritual. By inheritance Carter and his wife are members of the Church of England, but Virginia in the mid-18th century is filled with preachers: Baptists, Anabaptists, Methodists, Quakers, and Presbyterians are just a few of them. Carter listens to one after another, trying several faiths. In one 69-day period he attends 29 different religious services and hears 40 sermons. He becomes a friend to fellow seekers; some are black. One, his own half brother, is enslaved on his plantation.

Deeply impacted by the religious fundamentalism of the Great Awakening, Carter leads conservative thinkers to support

Frances Ann Tasker Carter, painted by John Wollaston (1755-58)

Jefferson's Statute for Religious Freedom. (It might not have passed without that support.)

Eventually he does what all his thinking contemporaries know is the right thing to do: he frees his enslaved workers (all 542 of them).

While Jefferson writes "all men are created equal," and calls slavery a "moral depravity" and a "hideous blot," he doesn't free his slaves. Nor does George Washington while he lives, and when some run away he has them chased. Washington's will manumits his slaves, but not his wife's. As for James Madison, writing to the Marquis de Lafayette in 1826, he says, "the two races cannot co-exist, both being free & equal." Madison believes and says that freed Africans should go back to the continent where they originated. He becomes a leader in a movement to send African Americans to Africa.

Slavery, as Seen by an Ex-Slave

"...I therefore hate the corrupt, slaveholding, women-whipping, cradle-plundering, partial and hypocritical Christianity of the land...We have men-stealers for ministers, women-whippers for missionaries, and cradle-plunderers for church members...The slave auctioneer's bell and the church-going bell chime in with each other, and the bitter cries of the heart-broken slave are drowned in the religious shouts of his pious master. Revivals of religion and revivals in the slave-trade go hand in hand together."

—Frederick Douglass, *Narrative of the Life of Frederick Douglass*

What's to be made of this? Could others have done what Robert Carter III did? Some of today's historians, rethinking the birth of the United States, believe that time offered a window for true freedom. (Later, after the cotton gin was developed and field workers were needed, it would become harder.)

Robert Carter III and his wife showed it could be done: they had more to lose than most slave owners, yet they freed more enslaved persons than anyone else in America. And they made sure that those they freed were able to support themselves.

It was a costly decision: they were hated and threatened by many of their peers. They had to move from their plantation to Baltimore. Their family was torn apart (some of their children were very angry).

Because Carter and his wife wouldn't accept what most of their peers were doing (holding people in slavery), their names got erased from history books. Carter asked to be buried in an unmarked grave (and he was). In a letter to his daughter Harriot, Carter wrote in 1803, "My plans and advice have never been pleasing to the world."

Robert Carter III did what he thought was the right thing to do. His wife supported him. Today most of us agree they were truly heroic.

To be fair...

Thomas Jefferson wasn't free to manumit his enslaved work force. At the end of his life he didn't own his workers or his plantation; his creditors did. That was not the case with Robert Carter III. Here are some details: Robert Carter was a brilliant businessman who had many plantations and grew a variety of crops. If one failed, another might prosper. He manufactured goods on his plantations and sold them elsewhere, he provided food and supplies for his workers, and he owned the means to ship and distribute his products. He owned an iron foundry. He loaned money to other planters and charged interest. Carter ran his plantations with great efficiency. Jefferson did not. Mostly he wasn't around to take charge; he was in Philadelphia writing a Declaration. He was in Paris being ambassador. He was in Washington being President. Jefferson had to borrow money to send to Monticello to keep his workers fed, to buy supplies needed to run the plantation. Robert Carter was among those who loaned him money. Read about capitalism and how borrowing is part of the way it works. But debts have to be paid. Jefferson tried hard to do that, but he couldn't.

Book Recommendation: *The Journal and Letters of Philip Vickers Fithian, 1773-1774: A Plantation Tutor of the Old Dominion*. When Robert Carter III decided to start a school for his children at his plantation, he hired Philip Fithian, who had just graduated from Princeton (then the College of New Jersey). Fithian kept a diary of his experience. Published as he wrote it, along with some of his letters, it is a thoughtful Northerner's look at 18th century plantation life. You will like Fithian and this wonderful book.

21 Why a National Cathedral in the Land of Diversity?

In 1792 Washington's architect, Pierre L'Enfant, asked Congress to set aside land for "a church intended for national purposes... assigned to the special use of no particular sect or denomination but equally open to all."

That church was never built (the land was used to build the National Portrait Gallery). But the city of Washington did become home to a National Cathedral: a huge Episcopal church standing on high ground in northwest Washington with spectacular views of the city that surrounds it. It's a Gothic structure, which means it has stained glass windows, high arches, and a gorgeous "rose" window, following an opulent architectural style that evolved in Europe beginning in the 12th century.

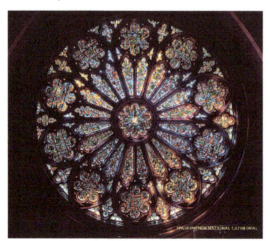

Today the National Cathedral is an active Protestant church holding regular Episcopal services, but it has also served as a place of worship and state functions for diverse Americans. Its story tells you a lot about the United States, the intention of its founding generation, the flexibility of those who have followed, and the spirituality of Americans of all faiths (and none).

Martin Luther King preached his last sermon at the National Cathedral. In 2014 carpeting was laid in a nave for Muslim prayers. It may not be exactly what Pierre L'Enfant intended, but it's not a bad compromise.

It took almost 100 years to build the church. The west towers were still under construction in the 1980s when a student competition was held for a new gargoyle.

Gargoyles are waterspouts designed as grotesque creatures. Those creatures are a heritage from medieval churches and were intended to ward off evil spirits. A high school student, Christopher Rader, was one of the winners of the 20th century competition when he made Darth Vader a gargoyle. The *Star Wars* villain was placed on the north or "dark side" of the Cathedral.

John F. Kennedy's Address to Protestant Ministers

September 12, 1960

John F. Kennedy was a candidate for president when he gave a speech to a group of Protestant Ministers in Houston, Texas. Many were concerned that his Roman Catholic faith would not allow him to make decisions without the consent of the Pope. Here is some of what he said. You can find the whole speech on the web.

Reverend Meza, Reverend Reck, I'm grateful for your generous invitation to speak my views.

While the so-called religious issue is necessarily and properly the chief topic here tonight, I want to emphasize from the outset that we have far more critical issues to face in the 1960 election; the spread of Communist influence, until it now festers 90 miles off the coast of Florida—the humiliating treatment of our President and Vice President by those who no longer respect our power—the hungry children I saw in West Virginia, the old people who cannot pay their doctor bills, the families forced to give up their farms—an America with too many slums, with too few schools, and too late to the moon and outer space.

These are the real issues which should decide this campaign. And they are not religious issues—for war and hunger and ignorance and despair know no religious barriers.

But because I am a Catholic, and no Catholic has ever been elected President, the real issues in this campaign have been obscured—perhaps deliberately, in some quarters less responsible than this. So it is apparently necessary for me to state once again—not what kind of church I believe in, for that should be important only to me—but what kind of America I believe in.

I believe in an America where the separation of church and state is absolute—where no Catholic prelate would tell the President (should he be Catholic) how to act, and no Protestant minister would tell his parishioners for whom to vote, where no church or church school is granted any public funds or political preference—and where no man is denied public office merely because his religion differs from the President who might appoint him or the people who might elect him.

I believe in an America that is officially neither Catholic, Protestant nor Jewish—where no public official either requests or accepts instructions on public policy from the Pope, the National Council of Churches or any other ecclesiastical source—where no religious body seeks to impose its will directly or indirectly upon the general populace or the public acts of its officials—and where religious liberty is so indivisible that an act against one church is treated as an act against all.

For while this year it may be a Catholic against whom the finger of suspicion is pointed, in other years it has been, and may someday be again, a Jew—or a Quaker—or a Unitarian—or a Baptist. It was Virginia's harassment of Baptist preachers, for example, that helped lead to Jefferson's statute of religious freedom. Today I may be the victim—but tomorrow it may be you—until the whole fabric of our harmonious society is ripped at a time of great national peril.

Finally, I believe in an America where religious intolerance will someday end—where all men and all churches are treated as equal—where every man has the same right to attend or not attend the church of his choice—where there is no Catholic vote, no anti-Catholic vote, no bloc voting of any kind—and where Catholics, Protestants and Jews, at both the lay and pastoral level, will refrain from those attitudes of disdain and division which have so often marred their works in the past, and promote instead the American ideal of brotherhood.

That is the kind of America in which I believe. And it represents the kind of Presidency in which I believe—a great office that must neither be humbled by making it the instrument of any one religious group nor tarnished by arbitrarily withholding its occupancy from the members of any one religious group. I believe in a President whose religious views are his own private affair, neither imposed by him upon the nation or imposed by the nation upon him as a condition to holding that office.

...

This is the kind of America I believe in—and this is the kind I fought for in the South Pacific, and the kind my brother died for in Europe. No one suggested then that we may have a "divided loyalty," that we did "not believe in liberty," or that we belonged to a disloyal group that threatened the "freedoms for which our forefathers died."

And in fact this is the kind of America for which our forefathers died—when they fled here to escape religious test oaths that denied office to members of less favored churches—when they fought for the Constitution, the Bill of Rights, and the Virginia Statute of Religious Freedom—and when they fought at the shrine I visited today, the Alamo. For side by side with Bowie and Crockett died McCafferty and Bailey and Carey—but no one knows whether they were Catholic or not. For there was no religious test at the Alamo.

…

I am not the Catholic candidate for President. I am the Democratic Party's candidate for President who happens also to be a Catholic. I do not speak for my church on public matters—and the church does not speak for me.

Whatever issue may come before me as President—on birth control, divorce, censorship, gambling or any other subject—I will make my decision in accordance with these views, in accordance with what my conscience tells me to be the national interest, and without regard to outside religious pressures or dictates. And no power or threat of punishment could cause me to decide otherwise.

…

If I should lose on the real issues, I shall return to my seat in the Senate, satisfied that I had tried my best and was fairly judged. But if this election is decided on the basis that 40 million Americans lost their chance of being President on the day they were baptized, then it is the whole nation that will be the loser, in the eyes of Catholics and non-Catholics around the world, in the eyes of history, and in the eyes of our own people.
But if, on the other hand, I should win the election, then I shall devote every effort of mind and spirit to fulfilling the oath of the Presidency—practically identical, I might add, to the oath I have taken for 14 years in the Congress. For without reservation, I can "solemnly swear that I will faithfully execute the office of President of the United States, and will to the best of my ability preserve, protect, and defend the Constitution . . . so help me God.

22 There's More to This Story

"Oh, East is East, and West is West, and the never the two shall meet,
Till Earth and Sky stand presently at God's great Judgment Seat;
— Rudyard Kipling, 1889

You may have noticed something missing from this book. It doesn't mention Hinduism, Buddishm, Taoism, Confucianism, Shinto, Jainism, and SIkhism. These are all major religions. A whole lot of the world's people follow them, so why aren't they included?

The reason is because they are religions centered in the Eastern world and for much of human history the world has been separated into Eastern and Western civilizations, with Jerusalem as a dividing point. We in the United States are part of what is known as Western civilization.

Books titled "Western history" usually begin in Jerusalem, or Egypt, or Greece, or Rome. From there they head north, to an emerging Europe. The ideas that we in the United States use as a base for our national beliefs come mostly from these regions.

Western religions are often called "Abrahamic." Judaism, Christianity, and Islam all use the Hebrew Bible as a base and celebrate its founding tale of Abraham and his son Isaac. While these three religions have adherents around the globe, Christianity, the world's largest religion, has its biggest following in the West.

That's not true of Islam. Many Muslims live in South Asia, and about 13% of all Muslims live in Indonesia; other large Muslim populations can be found in the Middle East and in Africa below the Sahara desert, as well as in Europe and the United States.

In the lands east of Jerusalem people developed their own ideas, wrote their own history books, and built their own religions. Did East and West communicate with each other? Those living in border regions did; so did merchants carrying goods to far places, and a few daring explorers. But before there were airplanes, traveling from East to West could take months, or years. As for telephoning? There were no phones, no internet, and no photography. So most people didn't know much of anything about those on the other side of the globe.

Rudyard Kipling was right. East was East and West was West, and rarely the twain did meet. As for religion, before this Information Age it was apt to be regional.

Today communication is easy and the divisions between East and West are vanishing. We are all becoming inhabitants of one world. What will that do to our beliefs? No one knows. Pay attention as the next chapter of the world's faith story unfolds. Will there be religious wars? History tells us that given freedom of belief there is no need to fight.

Part III

If you want to go further...

This is where you turn into a historian. Which means you need to do some research and then create something based on what you learn. It might be:

... a story
... a work of art
... a scholarly history
... a journal
... you might make and share a video.

It's your choice.

23 Reading and being Historians

Do you want to be a historian and research the past? Here is one way to get started: find a good history book that takes the subject you are interested in and puts it into the big picture of its time.

Check resources on the Internet. Be wary that most historians have reservations about Wikipedia! Nevertheless, it's a great place to start. Where you can, look for original documents.

Read what several historians have to say about the subject. We have been lucky with American history: we have now and have had in the past some fine historians writing about subjects like the Puritans, the Civil War, and most of our history. Don't make the mistake of thinking just because they may have published some years ago that they aren't worth reading. The latest publishing date does not mean the best.

Then try and digest all this material, find some words you might like to quote, and put all this into a package that will become your first draft (good writing usually takes many drafts).

As for historians to read: Perry Miller, writing in the 20th century, offered new insights about the Puritans. He is not easy, but usually worth the effort. Here's an excerpt from his book *Errand Into the Wilderness* that helps explain Puritan stubbornness.

> "When the Puritans came to New England the idea
> had not yet dawned that a government could safely

permit several creeds to exist side by side within the confines of a single nation. They had not beenfighting in England for any milk-and-water toleration, and had they been offered such religious freedom as dissenters now enjoy in Great Britain they would have scorned to accept the terms… The Puritans were assured that they alone knew the exact truth, as it was contained in the written word of God, and they were fighting to enthrone it in England and to extirpate utterly and mercilessly all other pretended versions of Christianity. When they could not succeed at home, they came to America, where they could establish a society in which the one and only truth should reign forever."

Extirpate? It means to get rid of by every legal means possible. Some synonyms are: weed out, destroy, eradicate, stamp out, root out, wipe out, eliminate, suppress, crush, put down, put an end to, get rid of. What would you like to extirpate? Are there people today who believe they know the "one and only truth?" Why is that often dangerous?

Here's a bit more from Perry Miller:

"It is almost pathetic to trace the puzzlement of New England leaders at the end of the seventeenth century, when the idea of toleration was becoming more and more respectable in European thought. They could hardly understand what was happening in their world, and they could not for a long time be persuaded that they had any reason to be ashamed of their record of so many Quakers whipped, blasphemers punished by the amputation of ears, Antinomians exiled, Anabaptists fined, or witches executed. By all the lights which had prevailed in Europe at the time the Puritans had left, these were achievements to which any government could point with pride."

Henry Steele Commager was a 20th century historian who specialized in intellectual (idea-centered) American history and wrote 40 books and 700 essays. He taught at New York University, Columbia University, and Amherst College. He was an eloquent spokesman when it came to the separation of church and state in America. Here is some of what he said:

> "We tend to forget that the separation of Church and State and the rejection of religious establishments was, in the eyes of the 18th century world, the most revolutionary experiment on which the new United States embarked. It commanded more attention, more applause and more censure than either the creation of a new nation, or the substitution of the coordinated State for Colonialism. No other western nation had ever attempted so reckless an experiment."

> "But the Founding Fathers knew what they were about: they wanted peace and harmony in a society dangerously heterogeneous which, even in the 18th century, confessed more than a score of denominations. They did not resort to subtle arguments or to elaborate legal provisions, but contented themselves with a general principle— one subject, as Madison observed, to a variety of interpretations. The principle itself was clear enough. John Adams put it bluntly: 'Congress shall never meddle with religion other than to say their own prayers and to give thanks once a year.' So, too, Madison asserted that, 'the Constitution does not create a shadow of a right in the general government to intermeddle with religion.'"

24 Who Are We?

Finding Our Stories

1. What do you know of your ancestors? If you interview your parents, grandparents, and relatives you'll discover that every one of them has a story. Record some of those stories and you have oral histories. President John F. Kennedy said we are "a Nation of Immigrants." All of us came to this land from elsewhere: Native Americans may have been first, but they came to America from Asia.

2. Most of us think that other people's families have interesting stories, but not ours. Don't be fooled. It's not only the rich and famous that have tales to tell. Everyone's story has meaning and surprises.

3. Finding your stories:
   Can you construct your family tree?
   Can you write about your roots?
   Why and when did your family come to America? Find out.
   Did your family have an easy time when they arrived? Why? Why not?
   Are you a Native American? Where are your tribal origins? Find out all you can about your heritage.
   Did your family arrive on a slave ship? It took strength and courage to survive the slave voyage and slavery itself. What can your family tell you about slavery? About your ancestors?
   Do charts, stories, a book.

4. Use your ethnic story creatively in art, music, or writing: try a mural, an oratorio, or a play. Compile your tales into a class book.

5. Sharing your heritage with others:
Class discussions, speeches, published works (self-publishing is fine).
Does discussing your heritage bother you? Is it an invasion of your privacy? Then find someone in your community and see if they'll let you tell their story.

6. How does your class's diversity compare with the rest of the community? How does your community compare with the country at large?
Use statistics in a research paper.

7. Does your class have a calendar showing religious holidays?
Are you sensitive to their importance?

8. Are you an immigrant?
Write about your experience coming to a new country. It may help your classmates understand the joys and traumas that their parents or grandparents endured.

9. Prepare a travel map of your journey to America or an ancestor's journey. Use it as a base for a paper—fiction or fact.

10. Are you aware of prejudice in school? Are some students made to feel like outsiders? Is there prejudice in your community? What can you do about it?

11. Do reports on the contributions of minorities to American culture.
Consider: Albert Einstein, Martin Luther King, I.M. Pei, Toni Morrison, Sonya Sotomayor, and someone you know.

Check the origins of authors, musicians, artists, and entertainers that you admire.

12. Read books on other cultures, especially biographies and autobiographies. Make a book list.

13. Find stories on prejudice and other experiences: Shakespeare's *Romeo and Juliet*, Bernstein/Sondheim's *West Side Story* (a modern retelling of the previous!), Maya Angelou's *I Know Why the Caged Bird Sings*, Claude Brown's *Manchild In the Promised Land*, Elie Wiesel's *Night*, Margaret Walker's *Jubilee*, Hal Borland's *When the Legends Die*, Harper Lee's *To Kill a Mockingbird*... (just to name a few)

14. What happens in a nation when individual rights are sacrificed for the "good of all?" (for example, the Holocaust, Russia under Stalin, today's Iran and North Korea, Puritan Massachusetts). Read Arthur Koestler's *Darkness At Noon*.

15. What do we mean by human rights? How are they abused today? Where? What about women's rights? Why did Malala Yousafzai win a Nobel Prize? Find out about Amnesty International and other international peace efforts.

16. What is an underdog? Does being an underdog mean your cause is right? Or wrong?

25 Visiting a University

Colleges and universities are eager to meet you. Most will give you a campus tour and answer your questions.

For those of us interested in religious freedom in America (and I hope that includes you), there is one university that stands above all the others and is well worth a visit. It's Mr. Jefferson's school, the University of Virginia in the lush Blue Ridge Mountains. Thomas Jefferson, a serious student of architecture, drew plans for that school in 1819, placing it a trot away from his spectacular hilltop home, Monticello.

Home and school are both near the village of Charlottesville, which if you could fly on a bird's back is 107.8 kilometers (or 67 miles) from Virginia's capital city Richmond. Jefferson, who served as Virginia's governor, had to ride horseback on an Indian hunting path to get home. It usually took him two days. When Charlottesville became a city in 1888 (Jefferson died on the 4th of July in 1826) the Indian path had become Three-Notched Road and ran right through the middle of the town (it's now the site of Downtown Mall).

Thomas Jefferson, aware he was taking part in the building of a new nation, felt a great responsibility to his contemporaries and also to future generations. He wanted the new nation to be built on great ideas, the best to be found. He saw architecture as a way to tie those ideas to exceptional structures. Architectural design, he believed, could and should reflect a nation's ideals.

"academical village." Then he designed an imposing rotunda, a round building inspired by the work of the great Italian Renaissance architect Andrea Palladio (who is worth researching); it overlooks a great lawn with pavilions, common spaces, and student rooms.

Today a famous statue of Jefferson done by sculptor Moses Ezekiel stands on one side of the rotunda. Ezekiel, who was the first Jewish graduate of Virginia Military Academy, roomed there with Jefferson's great nephew. They became best friends and fought together in the Civil War. Growing up in 19th century Richmond, Ezekiel faced anti-Semitism, which may be why he thought that religious liberty was the greatest of the founding generation's achievements. It may explain why four spirits surround the statue; they are Justice, Liberty, Equality, and Religious Freedom. And also why Ezekiel carved the names of these religious icons on a tablet that is part of the structure: Jehovah, Allah, Brahma, Ra, Atman, Zeus, and God.

Moses Ezekiel said he carved the deity names to show that "under our government they mean and are all God... and have each an equal right and protection of our just laws as Americans."

Words, Words, Words

There is a key word on these pages: it is **pluralism**.

If you take it apart—into "plural-" and "-ism"—you can see it has something to do with more than one.

The dictionary says pluralism means: a condition of society in which many distinct ethnic, religious, or cultural groups coexist within one nation.

Which, in simple words, means: if you have citizens whose origins are Polish and Greek and Italian and Japanese and African—as we do in the United States—then you are a pluralistic nation.

If you have citizens who are Methodist and Hindu and Jewish and Catholic and Buddhist—as we do in the United States—you have a pluralistic nation.

There are other words that convey a plural or multiple meaning. They are not all exact synonyms, but they all have to do with mixtures.

diverse
multiplicity
varied
hodgepodge
dissimilar
multiracial
sundry

Two words with interesting stories: **heterogeneous** and **polyglot**.

Heterogeneous usually means a mixture of unrelated parts. Itssynonyms are: varied, diverse, assorted, or mixed up. That's in contrast to **homogeneous**, where the parts are all the same or closely related. Synonyms of homogeneous are: consistent, uniform, harmonious, similar. Both of these words can be used in chemistry to describe mixtures. So heterogeneous is the opposite of homogeneous. What is homogeneous? Something that is alike in all its parts. Today there are no completely homogeneous nations, but Japan comes close. Most of its citizens are of Japanese origin. Some other nations, like Sweden, have traditionally been homogeneous (today that is changing). In the United States we are and always have been a heterogeneous nation—we're all mixed up!

About word origins: *heteros*, from Greek, means "other." And *genus*, from Latin, means "race or kind."

Polyglot is an unusual, strange-sounding word that comes from two Greek roots: *poly* meaning "more than one," and *glossa* meaning "tongue."

So a polyglot nation is one where you can hear many tongues (languages) spoken.

The United States is a polyglot nation. New York is a polyglot city. Today, most big cities are polyglot.

While we are considering word origins, *glossa* gives us glossary. *Poly* is the root of many, many English words. Just look in a dictionary; you'll be amazed.

How about making your own list of poly words?

Is this getting a bit heavy? Well, here is one more, a word you can use in France or America. It has the same meaning and the same pronunciation in two languages, French and English. The word is melange (may-lahnge.)

The French put an accent over the é: mélange. In French it means—this should be no surprise—a mixture.

If you haven't had enough, just look up "mixture" in a thesaurus. You'll find many other related words.

A few more words to consider: **abhorred**, **suppressed**, **pious**, **dissenters**.

For Further Study

A Few Ideas for Class Reports, Papers, Or Additional Reading and Class Discussion

Galileo Galilei

The Italian astronomer and physicist was a contemporary of the Puritans. Galileo became the center of a momentous conflict between the Roman Catholic Church and the new ideas coming from scientific thinkers. Galileo supported the concept—first put forth by Poland's Nicholaus Copernicus—that the earth revolves around the sun, not vice versa as most people believed. In 1632, Galileo was called before the Inquisition, which was a Church body formed to find and punish heretics (those who challenged Church doctrine). Church officials forced Galileo to renounce the Copernican theory and then sentenced him to life imprisonment at his home in Florence.

Mahatma Gandhi

Can a political hero also be a religious leader? Mahatma Gandhi filled both roles. He was a Hindu who helped his nation, India, become free of British rule and he did it through nonviolent means. He would inspire others, especially Martin Luther King, Jr., to denounce violence. Gandhi wanted Hindus and Muslims to live together in India. But he was challenged by others with different visions. Read his story and make up your own mind about the issues he championed.

John Milton

The great English poet was a deeply religious friend of Roger Williams. He said a writer "ought himself to be a true poem" and tried to live a righteous life. When he was young he thought he would be a minister, but he found that "tyranny had invaded the church." He wrote pamphlets in favor of freedom of the press and the right of people to choose their own rulers—ideas far ahead of his times. Every educated American in the 17th and 18th centuries was familiar with Milton's work: most had read his great poem *Paradise Lost*. Many were aware of the speech he gave in 1644 defending press freedom and opposing censorship. It is titled *Aeropagitica*. His thoughts on religious liberty were not as establishment as those of John Winthrop nor as groundbreaking as those of Roger Williams.

John Locke

Locke, an English political philosopher, was born the year Galileo was brought before the Roman Catholic Church court called the Inquisition. Although he lived in the 17th century, his ideas profoundly influenced the thinkers of the next century. Locke believed in freedom of thought and religion, for both moral and practical reasons. If you know about John Locke you will more easily understand Thomas Jefferson and his generation.

OTHER IDEAS AND PEOPLE TO STUDY and maybe write about

The Salem Witchcraft Trials
The Great Awakening (revivalism in 1730-1740)
Jonathan Edwards
Samuel Davies
Francis Asbury
John Winthrop
John Cotton
Increase Mather
Isaac Backus
Martin Luther King, Jr.
Islam in 21st century America
The Scopes trial

Judaism in the US

The African Methodist Episcopal Church Atheism in the US

The growth of Islam and other non-Christian religions in America

The history of your own place of worship (if you have one) A 21st century Pope: Francis

Stories behind Supreme Court cases on religious liberty

Image Credits

Chapter 4

Martin Luther, Lucas Cranach the Elder; public domain.

Burning of Three Witches in Baden, Switzerland by Johann Jacob Wick; public domain.

Robert Hooke's drawing of a flea; public domain; Wikipedia.org.

King James I by John de Critz the Elder; public domain.

Model of a 17th C Merchant vessel, Dorset County Museum by User Musphot on Wikimedia Commons.

Landing of the Pilgrims at Plymouth, 19th century engraving; Library of Congress.

Chapter 5

A Wanton Gospeller, engraving, artist unknown; New England Historical Society.

Chapter 6

Roger Williams; Wikimedia Commons.

Chapter 7

Print by Carel Allard is after a painting by Egbert van Heemskerk circa 1675; public domain.

Mary Dyer; unknown 19th century artist; public domain.

Chapter 8

Peter Stuyvesant and the Trumpeter, Asher B. Durand (1796-1886), 1835. Oil on canvas. New-York Historical Society, Gift of the New York Gallery of the Fine Arts.

Chapter 9

Flushing Remonstrance, DC Comics, cover-dated 1970. Published as a public service in cooperation with the National Social Welfare Assembly.

Flushing Remonstrance fragment, New York State Library.

Chapter 10

Monument "Road of Slaves;" Wikimedia Commons.

Portrait of Diallo, (also known as Job ben Solomon), William Hoare, 1733. Public domain.

Chapter 11

Ark and Dove commemorative stamp, U.S. Postal Service 1934.

Wikipedia.org.

Woodcut, *Execution of Charles 1*; public domain.

Chapter 12

The Birth of Pennsylvania 1680 by Jean Leon Gerome Ferris; public domain.

Chapter 14

Whitefield Preaching, engraving circa 1740. The Granger Collection, NYC.

Mrs. Juliann Jane Tillman, Preacher of the A.M.E. Church by Alfred M. Hoffy; Library of Congress.

Detail, Phillis Wheatley, *Boston Women's Memorial*, Meredith Bergmann; photo, Wikipedia.org.

Chapter 15

The Reverend Lemuel Haynes Preaching, c. 1810, unknown artist. Wikimedia Commons.

Lemuel Haynes home, Wikipedia.org.

Chapter 17

Thomas Jefferson, Rembrandt Peale; Wikimedia Commons.

Thomas Jefferson grave at Monticello; Wikimedia Commons.

Chapter 19

Camp Meeting Plan, Benjamin Latrobe, c. 1809. Library of Congress.

Chapter 20

Robert Carter III of Nomini Hall. Thomas Hudson, 1753. Public domain.

Portrait of Frances Ann Tasker Carter (Mrs. Robert Carter III). 1755-58, attributed to John Wollaston. Courtesy Colonial Williamsburg, (public domain).

Chapter 21

Rose Window: W. Geiger, Washington National Cathedral. Darth Vader gargoyle: C. Winterbottom, Washington National Cathedral.

Chapter 25

Thomas Jefferson statue, detail *Vox Populi, Vox Dei*; Moses Ezekiel c. 1910. Photo, Wikimedia Commons.

CPSIA information can be obtained
at www.ICGtesting.com
Printed in the USA
BVHW060940220419
546161BV00015B/448/P